Columbia University

Contributions to Education

Teachers College Series

No. 517

AMS PRESS
NEW YORK

LEARNING AND APPLYING SPELLING RULES IN GRADES THREE TO EIGHT

BY

LUELLA M. KING

SUBMITTED IN PARTIAL FULFILLMENT OF THE REQUIREMENTS FOR
THE DEGREE OF DOCTOR OF PHILOSOPHY IN THE FACULTY
OF PHILOSOPHY, COLUMBIA UNIVERSITY

*Published with the approval
of Professor Arthur I. Gates, Sponsor*

219488

BUREAU OF PUBLICATIONS
Teachers College, Columbia University
NEW YORK CITY
1932

Library of Congress Cataloging in Publication Data

King, Luella Myrtle, 1887-
    Learning and applying spelling rules in grades three
to eight.

    Reprint of the 1932 ed., issued in series: Teachers
College, Columbia University. Contributions to education, no. 517.
    Originally presented as the author's thesis, Colum-
bia.
    Bibliography: p.
    1. English language--Orthography and spelling.
2. English language--Study and teaching (Elementary)
--United States. I. Title. II. Series: Columbia
University. Teachers College. Contributions to education, no. 517.

LB1574.K5 1972   372.6'32   72-7937
ISBN 0-404-55517-9

Reprinted by Special Arrangement with Teachers
College Press, New York, New York

From the edition of 1932, New York
First AMS edition published in 1972
Manufactured in the United States

AMS PRESS, INC.
NEW YORK, N. Y.   10003

ACKNOWLEDGMENTS

The author takes this occasion to express her appreciation of the assistance and encouragement without which this study could not have been made. Many members of the faculty of Teachers College, Columbia University, have contributed to whatever success has been attained. In particular, Professors Arthur I. Gates, Mary T. Whitley, and Edwin H. Reeder were unfailing in their responses to appeals for help. Professor Gates gave invaluable advice throughout the experiment. The librarians at Teachers College made many concessions in order that the necessary reading material might be available. Miss Gertrude L. Belser, Secretary of the Committee on Higher Degrees at Teachers College, was equal to all emergencies. Finally, a debt of gratitude is owed to the teachers, the pupils, and the administrative staff of the Garden City School for their sympathetic coöperation and interest throughout the experimental work.

L. M. K.

CONTENTS

CHAPTER   PAGE

I. SOME OPINIONS AND RESEARCHES RELATED TO TEACHING
RULES IN SPELLING 1

II. GENERAL CHARACTER OF THIS EXPERIMENT 6

III. SELECTION OF RULES 7

IV. TEACHING THE RULES 12

V. INTERPRETATION OF RESULTS OF FINAL EXAMINATIONS
ON RULES 17

VI. SUMMARY AND CONCLUSIONS 60

APPENDIX

I. TEST ON PRELIMINARY TERMS 65

II. SAMPLE LESSON PLANS FOR RULES VII AND IV 66

III. FINAL EXAMINATIONS ON RULES I, II, III, V, AND VI.. 75

BIBLIOGRAPHY.. 79

TABLES

TABLE   PAGE

1. Frequency of Application and Exceptions for Each Rule by Grades According to the Gates-Graham List 8

2. Percentage of Errors in Spelling *sts* Plurals 10

3. Showing Grade Distribution and Number of Lessons for Each Rule .. 14

4. Distribution by Grades of Mental Age of Children 17

5. Rule I—Plurals in *s* and *es*. Distribution by Grades of Percentage of Children Receiving Each Score on the Examination as a Whole .. 18

6. Rule I—Plurals in *s* and *es*. Distribution by Grades of Percentage of Children Receiving Each Score on the Statement of the Rule 19

7. Rule I—Plurals in *s* and *es*. Distribution by Grades of Percentage of Children Receiving Each Score on Spelling Real Words 19

8. Rule I—Plurals in *s* and *es*. Distribution by Grades of Percentage of Children Receiving Each Score on Spelling Nonsense Words 20

9. Rule I—Plurals in *s* and *es*. Distribution by Mental Ages of Percentage of Children Receiving Each Score on the Examination as a Whole 21

10. Rule I—Plurals in *s* and *es*. Distribution by Mental Ages of Percentage of Children Receiving Each Score on the Statement of the Rule 22

11. Rule I—Plurals in *s* and *es*. Distribution by Mental Ages of Percentage of Children Receiving Each Score on Spelling Real Words 22

12. Rule I—Plurals in *s* and *es*. Distribution by Mental Ages of Percentage of Children Receiving Each Score on Spelling Nonsense Words .. 23

13. Rule II—Dropping Final *e*. Distribution by Grades of Percentage of Children Receiving Each Score on the Examination as a Whole 25

14. Rule II—Dropping Final *e*. Distribution by Grades of Percentage of Children Receiving Each Score on the Statement of the Rule 25

15. Rule II—Dropping Final *e*. Distribution by Grades of Percentage of Children Receiving Each Score on Spelling Real Words 26

16. Rule II—Dropping Final *e*. Distribution by Grades of Percentage of Children Receiving Each Score on Spelling Nonsense Words 26

17. Rule II—Dropping Final *e*. Distribution by Mental Ages of Percentage of Children Receiving Each Score on the Examination as a Whole 27

18. Rule II—Dropping Final *e*. Distribution by Mental Ages of Percentage of Children Receiving Each Score on the Statement of the Rule .. 28

19. Rule II—Dropping Final *e*. Distribution by Mental Ages of Percentage of Children Receiving Each Score on Spelling Real Words 28

20. Rule II—Dropping Final *e*. Distribution by Mental Ages of Percentage of Children Receiving Each Score on Spelling Nonsense Words .. 29

TABLE   PAGE

21. Rule III—Changing *y* to *i*. Distribution by Grades of Percentage of Children Receiving Each Score on the Examination as a Whole 31

22. Rule III—Changing *y* to *i*. Distribution by Grades of Percentage of Children Receiving Each Score on the Statement of the Rule 32

23. Rule III—Changing *y* to *i*. Distribution by Grades of Percentage of Children Receiving Each Score on Spelling Real Words 32

24. Rule III—Changing *y* to *i*. Distribution by Grades of Percentage of Children Receiving Each Score on Spelling Nonsense Words 33

25. Rule III—Changing *y* to *i*. Distribution by Mental Ages of Percentage of Children Receiving Each Score on the Examination as a Whole 34

26. Rule III—Changing *y* to *i*. Distribution by Mental Ages of Percentage of Children Receiving Each Score on the Statement of the Rule . 35

27. Rule III—Changing *y* to *i*. Distribution by Mental Ages of Percentage of Children Receiving Each Score on Spelling Real Words 35

28. Rule III—Changing *y* to *i*. Distribution by Mental Ages of Percentage of Children Receiving Each Score on Spelling Nonsense Words .. 36

29. Rule IV—*Qu*. Distribution by Grades of Percentage of Children Receiving Each Score on the Examination as a Whole 38

30. Rule IV—*Qu*. Distribution by Grades of Percentage of Children Receiving Each Score on the Statement of the Rule 38

31. Rule IV—*Qu*. Distribution by Grades of Percentage of Children Receiving Each Score on Spelling Real Words 39

32. Rule IV—*Qu*. Distribution by Grades of Percentage of Children Receiving Each Score on Spelling Nonsense Words 39

33. Rule IV—*Qu*. Distribution by Mental Ages of Percentage of Children Receiving Each Score on the Examination as a Whole 40

34. Rule IV—*Qu*. Distribution by Mental Ages of Percentage of Children Receiving Each Score on the Statement of the Rule 40

35. Rule IV—*Qu*. Distribution by Mental Ages of Percentage of Children Receiving Each Score on Spelling Real Words 41

36. Rule IV—*Qu*. Distribution by Mental Ages of Percentage of Children Receiving Each Score on Spelling Nonsense Words 41

37. Rule V—*Ie* and *ei*. Distribution by Grades of Percentage of Children Receiving Each Score on the Examination as a Whole 43

38. Rule V—*Ie* and *ei*. Distribution by Grades of Percentage of Children Receiving Each Score on the Statement of the Rule 43

39. Rule V—*Ie* and *ei*. Distribution by Grades of Percentage of Children Receiving Each Score on Spelling Real Words 44

40. Rule V—*Ie* and *ei*. Distribution by Grades of Percentage of Children Receiving Each Score on Spelling Nonsense Words 44

41. Rule V—*Ie* and *ei*. Distribution by Mental Ages of Percentage of Children Receiving Each Score on the Examination as a Whole 45

42. Rule V—*Ie* and *ei*. Distribution by Mental Ages of Percentage of Children Receiving Each Score on the Statement of the Rule 46

TABLE   PAGE

43. Rule V—*Ie* and *ei*. Distribution by Mental Ages of Percentage of Children Receiving Each Score on Spelling Real Words 46

44. Rule V—*Ie* and *ei*. Distribution by Mental Ages of Percentage of Children Receiving Each Score on Spelling Nonsense Words 47

45. Rule VI—Sound of *i* Spelled *y*. Distribution by Grades of Percentage of Children Receiving Each Score on the Examination as a Whole ... 48

46. Rule VI—Sound of *i* Spelled *y*. Distribution by Grades of Percentage of Children Receiving Each Score on the Statement of the Rule 49

47. Rule VI—Sound of *i* Spelled *y*. Distribution by Grades of Percentage of Children Receiving Each Score on Spelling Real Words 49

48. Rule VI—Sound of *i* Spelled *y*. Distribution by Grades of Percentage of Children Receiving Each Score on Spelling Nonsense Words 50

49. Rule VI—Sound of *i* Spelled *y*. Distribution by Mental Ages of Percentage of Children Receiving Each Score on the Examination as a Whole.. 51

50. Rule VI—Sound of *i* Spelled *y*. Distribution by Mental Ages of Percentage of Children Receiving Each Score on the Statement of the Rule 52

51. Rule VI—Sound of *i* Spelled *y*. Distribution by Mental Ages of Percentage of Children Receiving Each Score on Spelling Real Words .. 52

52. Rule VI—Sound of *i* Spelled *y*. Distribution by Mental Ages of Percentage of Children Receiving Each Score on Spelling Nonsense Words 53

53. Rule VII—Doubling Final Consonant. Distribution by Grades of Percentage of Children Receiving Each Score on the Examination as a Whole.. 54

54. Rule VII—Doubling Final Consonant. Distribution by Grades of Percentage of Children Receiving Each Score on the Statement of the Rule 55

55. Rule VII—Doubling Final Consonant. Distribution by Grades of Percentage of Children Receiving Each Score on Spelling Real Words .. 55

56. Rule VII—Doubling Final Consonant. Distribution by Grades of Percentage of Children Receiving Each Score on Spelling Nonsense Words 56

57. Inefficiency of Spelling Nonsense Words Governed by Rule VII as Measured by the Per Cent of Possible Number of Errors Made 56

58. Rule VII—Doubling Final Consonant. Distribution by Mental Ages of Percentage of Children Receiving Each Score on the Examination as a Whole 57

59. Rule VII—Doubling Final Consonant. Distribution by Mental Ages of Percentage of Children Receiving Each Score on the Statement of the Rule 58

60. Rule VII—Doubling Final Consonant. Distribution by Mental Ages of Percentage of Children Receiving Each Score on Spelling Real Words 58

61. Rule VII—Doubling Final Consonant. Distribution by Mental Ages of Percentage of Children Receiving Each Score on Spelling Nonsense Words 59

LEARNING AND APPLYING SPELLING RULES IN GRADES THREE TO EIGHT

CHAPTER I

SOME OPINIONS AND RESEARCHES RELATED TO TEACHING RULES IN SPELLING

Recent reports of researches in the psychology of learning to spell have contained such excellent reviews of the development of the subject that this chapter aims to give only the general trend of these ideas as applied to the teaching of rules in spelling.

The work of Sartorius [13] on *Generalization in Spelling* devotes a chapter to the teaching of spelling rules as one form of generalization. The author gives an excellent résumé of the views of experts on the subject. Since her topic is so closely related to the present one, any discussion of opinions and researches in this field must overlap her discussion. [pp. 1-7]

At present the teaching of rules in spelling seems to be emerging from the "all or none" acceptance of a theory that has characterized the various phases of teaching. This attitude has been pronounced with respect to the value of rules. A chronological survey of some of the expressions of opinions and findings of research will give an interesting view of this changing psychology.

In 1906 Burnham, writing of the work of Lay, said:

> As a result of his experiments and general study and observation, Lay draws several important, practical inferences, as follows: "cultivation of a correct pronunciation is of great importance for learning orthography. . . . The rules also are not directly of value but are important as a means of fixing the attention and arousing the critical sense for orthographic forms." [3, p. 487]

In 1912 Cook [5] reported an experiment with some college freshmen and high school students. The experiment aimed to test the value of rules that had been taught previously. There were seven rules in all. Cook's conclusion was that not a single rule tested proved to be of real value, except the one for the last two words of the list—that relating to the final *ie*. This rule says that words ending in *ie* change the *ie* to *y* before adding the suffix *ing*.

In the same year Turner [18] reported a study on "Rules Versus Drill in Teaching Spelling." He experimented with two groups of sixteen pupils each, chosen on the basis of grades secured in a common test in spelling. These were called a drill group and a rules group. The same test was given twice, once at the close of the last learning period and once five days later. In regard to the second test, Turner says that both groups showed a slight falling off in efficiency but that the drill group lost relatively less than the rules group.

A second set of words, new but similar to those in the first set, was given twice also, once at the end of the last teaching period, and once five days later. The test given at the end of the last teaching period was called test "D"; the one given five days later was called test "E." When the test of new words was first given, the rules group had a distinct advantage. Of the second testing Turner says:

> The drill group seems to have recovered the ground lost in the "D" test. The rules group gains a better average than in the "D" test, but the influence of the latter test is not so strongly marked as with the drill group. [p. 460]

In 1911 Suzzallo wrote:

> In progressive practice the teaching of rules has gone through about the same modifications as word-analysis. It was overdone twenty years ago, the reaction against formal deductive ways of teaching tending to eliminate it completely; now there is a tendency towards its restoration to a restricted place with a much changed emphasis and use. . . . The better books do not call for the memorization of many rules, with numerous exceptions, followed by a study of more or less unfamiliar illustrations. The teacher is quite content when the child merely senses the general principle, and refrains from any verbal formulation of the rule. [14, pp. 89-90]

In 1917 Lester, commenting on the conclusion reached by Cook and O'Shea that "not a single rule tested proved to be of value," said:

> Now the value of rules is not to be sought in the evidence of students who, as was the case of those investigated, had never really learned them. It is to be sought in the applicability of the rules to the problem in hand.

. . . Hence students should learn these rules as necessary tools with which to perform a piece of work. . . . The writer's experience is at absolute variance with the experience set forth by Cook and O'Shea. Students were required to memorize the five rules absolutely; and it was pointed out to them that . . . they were merely acquiring a tool ready at hand to use, and, having acquired the tool, they should use it. Eight weeks later the 75 students were asked to write a candid, unsigned statement as to whether they found the rules learned useful; 85 per cent replied "yes" to this question. This conclusion does not bear out the statement that "not a single rule tested proved to be of value." [11, p. 408]

In 1919 Horn [8] expressed the opinion that rules cannot replace direct instruction in spelling even in the case of words covered by them. He said:

Most of the articles dealing with the subject contain a peculiar fallacy, namely, that by discovering what words are covered by a given rule, one may discover the efficiency of teaching that rule. As a matter of fact, one must show in addition to the above that the rule can be easily taught, that it will be remembered, and that it will function in the stress of actual spelling. Evidence seems to cast a doubt on all three of these assumptions. . . .

It is desirable that someone investigate the result of teaching rules to the point where they are fixed and their use habituated. . . . In the light of present evidence one seems to be justified in recommending that the teaching of rules be abandoned until more conclusive evidence is presented to show that the time spent in teaching them is as productive of efficiency as the same amount of time spent in teaching the words directly. [p. 55]

Horn believes that it is necessary to teach derived forms in spelling, although they should not be taught by rules. In 1919 he and Ashbaugh [9] presented data to show "that in the great majority of cases a change in form is accompanied by a difference in spelling difficulty" [p. 143]; also "that in selecting words to make up the course of study in spelling each change in spelling should be incorporated as a separate word; . . . that in teaching these words each separate form should be taught as a different word." [p. 151]

In 1925 Watson [20] conducted two experiments in the teaching of spelling rules to high school classes. The first was with two B10 classes. This experiment compared the achievement of one group, which had received individual study, with access to formulated rules, with that of another group which had received individual drill. After twenty-five spelling periods of fifteen minutes each, the initial test was repeated. On this re-test 100 per cent of the students having access to rules reached or exceeded the median score of the initial test, while only 87.5 per cent of those having individual drill made a similar score.

In the second experiment the achievement of two B9 classes was compared. One group had received class study of spelling rules and the other had received class drill. After twenty-seven periods of fifteen minutes each, the initial test was repeated. One hundred per cent of the rules group equaled or exceeded the median of the initial test score. Eighty-eight per cent of the drill group made a similar score. In both experiments the groups having access to rules showed more improvement than the drill group. [pp. 507 ff.]

In 1924 Tidyman and Johnson [17] published a study on the value of grouping words according to similar difficulties in spelling. They concluded that "the results show the superiority of the grouping method not only in improvement but also in the average number of mistakes made per pupil in the ten learning lessons." [p. 297] This study supported a similar study made in 1912 by Wagner [19], who wrote that grouping words into lessons according to spelling difficulty secures better daily lessons, better final results, and greater steadiness or constancy of correct spelling. (See also Tidyman and Johnson [17].) Mendenhall, writing in 1930, added the weight of his opinion to the value of grouping words according to common spelling errors. [12, p. 52]

These three studies are related to spelling rules by the fact that they all deal with similarities. It is possible that rules may be found definitely helpful in emphasizing these elements of similarities.

The possibility of this use of rules was suggested by Gates and Chase [6] in their report of a study of spelling methods as tested with deaf children. They wrote:

> While the use of spelling rules has largely fallen into disrepute there are theoretical reasons and some experimental evidence tending to show that when used as one of the means of emphasizing the visible similarities and differences among groups of like and unlike forms they may be fruitfully employed to improve word-perceptive habits and, consequently, spelling ability. [p. 300]

In 1930 Carroll [4] made a comparative study of the generalizations of bright and dull children with special reference to spelling. He concluded that the psychological explanation of the differences in spelling errors made by the dull and the bright children was to be found in "the marked superiority of the bright over the dull in phonetic generalization ability." [p. 54]

In view of the conflicting opinions and research findings reviewed in this chapter, it is not surprising that we find Thorndike [16] writing in 1929 on "The Need of Fundamental Analysis of Methods of Teaching." In speaking of the unsatisfactory application of the facts and principles of educational psychology, he said:

> One element of remedy is more fundamental and thorough analysis of methods of teaching—of what happens when the learner is provided with such and such situations or stimuli and led by such and such means to respond in such and such ways. [p. 189]

After giving one illustration, Thorndike proceeded:

> As a second illustration, we may take the learning of English spelling. The leading expert in this field, Ernest Horn, relies almost entirely on the learning of the spelling of each word by itself, having almost no confidence in generalizations of any kind in this field. We may agree with him in his skepticism concerning the value of the ordinary rules and similarities as commonly taught and still hope that a more fundamental analysis will indicate certain combinations of generalization and one-by-one learning as superior to the latter alone. For example, the generalizations "*oa* is very common, *ao* is very rare, *ea* is very common, *ae* is very rare, *ee* is very common, *aa* is very rare" seem worth the minute or two it takes to make them. . . . Wholesale acceptance or rejection of any procedure is risky as a method of teaching. It is often necessary to extend the analysis to each case. [p. 190]

It is evident that no one has the answer to the question "Shall we teach rules in spelling?" In fact, this query is no longer helpful except as a point of departure. The question must be reduced to such specific elements as: what rules, to whom taught, how taught, and the comparative value of rules as a teaching method. Only as these and similar problems are investigated to such a degree that their solution will result in improved classroom practice can we have a satisfactory ending of this controversy.

CHAPTER II

GENERAL CHARACTER OF THIS EXPERIMENT

The research described in the present study was undertaken for the purpose of determining the effects of teaching certain spelling rules in each of several elementary grades. Suggestions concerning the fitness of the several rules for specific grades were sought in data relating to the frequency of application in the spelling words of a grade, to the distribution throughout the grades of words governed by these rules, to the number of exceptions, and to the ease of learning.

Seven rules were selected and taught by the teacher in charge to children in Grades 3 to 8 inclusive. Not all rules were used in all grades; all, however, followed the same general procedure.

The experimenter furnished rather detailed lesson plans and a final examination for each rule. Samples of these lessons and examinations are given in the Appendix. The lesson plans and the final examinations were the same for all grades except that the words given for introducing a rule, and used for drill usually consisted of three different lists. One list was given to Grades 3 and 4, one to Grades 5 and 6, and one to Grades 7 and 8.

The scores obtained in the examinations on the rules were tabulated both by grades and by mental ages. Tables were prepared showing the percentage of children of each grade and of each mental age receiving the various scores.

The final scores and the original test papers were then examined for suggestions which might apply to teaching. The kinds of errors and the frequency of each error were determined for each rule by grades. The obtained frequency of each error was related by percentage to the possible frequency of that error.

Finally an attempt was made to discover any facts that might be useful in the teaching of spelling. Any unusual conditions were noted and, if possible, accounted for. All important findings were summarized for ready reference.

CHAPTER III

SELECTION OF RULES

As stated in Chapter II, the spelling rules taught in the course of this experiment were selected on the basis of frequency of application to the spelling words of the elementary grades, their distribution throughout these grades, the number of exceptions to the rules, and the probable ease of learning.

These criteria were applied to an experimental list of spelling words prepared by Professor Arthur I. Gates and Mr. Frederick B. Graham. This list was used by Sartorius in her study on *Generalization in Spelling* [13]. In writing of its composition she says:

> The list was composed of all the words in the Ayres-Buckingham Spelling List, the first 5,000 words in the Horn Basic Vocabulary, the 2,916 word-forms in the Gates Primary Reading List, and all derived as well as basal forms of the first 4,000 words in the Thorndike Word List. These data were combined with all the words listed in the following seven spellers, which are believed to be so widely used in this country that they would represent the words studied in school by a very large proportion of children.
>
> 1. Horn-Ashbaugh Fundamentals of Spelling
> 2. Lippincott's New Horn-Ashbaugh Speller
> 3. The New York City List
> 4. Jones' Complete Course in Spelling
> 5. The McCall Speller
> 6. Smith-Bagley Mastery Speller
> 7. Breed-French Speller
>
> Since the 4,065 words selected represent those most commonly appearing in widely used spelling textbooks and those which appear with the greatest frequency in the best-known studies of children's usage, it is believed that they represent approximately the words most commonly taught in the first eight grades in this country and also those most commonly used by the children in these grades. [p. 10]

In selecting the rules for this study, the findings of Sartorius were consulted for frequency of application, spread throughout the grades, and for exceptions. Six of her rules were chosen for experimentation. To these was added another which was found in *The McCall Speller, Book Two*.

Table I gives the frequency of application and exceptions for each rule by grades. The items under Rule VI were tabulated by the writer from the Gates-Graham list. The rules are numbered according to the order in which they were taught. This is not the same numbering as that used by Sartorius.

TABLE 1

FREQUENCY OF APPLICATION AND EXCEPTIONS FOR EACH RULE BY GRADES
ACCORDING TO THE GATES-GRAHAM LIST

GRADE	RULE						
	I	II	III	IV	V	VI	VII
Grade 2	3	2	0		1	15	1
Grade 3	18	14	6		12	27	5
Grade 4	37	11	3	8	9	31	8
Grade 5	17	26	10	6	26	55	8
Grade 6	12	23	13	7	28	57	12
Grade 7	18	42	7	12	17	57	3
Grade 8	20	49	17	21	21	88	8
Total	125	167	56	54	114	330	45
Exceptions	25	4	1	0	17	20	13

The following are statements of the rules as used in the experimental lessons.

Rule I—Most nouns form their plurals by adding *s* or *es* to the singular. *Es* is added to make the word easier to pronounce.

Rule II—Drop the final *e* before adding a suffix beginning with a vowel.

Rule III—When final *y* is preceded by a consonant, change the *y* to *i* before adding any suffix that does not begin with *i*.

Rule IV—*Q* is always followed by *u*.

Rule V—*I* before *e*
　　　　Except after *c*
　　　　Or when sounded as ā
　　　　As in *neighbor* and *weigh*.

Rule VI—The sound of *i* at the end of a word is usually spelled by the letter *y*.

Rule VII—Words of one syllable and words with the accent on the last syllable ending in one consonant preceded by one vowel, double the final consonant when adding a suffix beginning with a vowel.

Table 1 shows that Rule I has a frequency of 125 scattered throughout Grades 2 to 8. Sartorius [13] reports that there are 25 words in the Gates-Graham list that do not form their plurals by adding *s* or *es* to the singular. Eight of these are gentlemen, men, mice, geese, teeth, women, leaves, and lives. Sixteen exceptions are words ending in final *y* preceded by a consonant and forming their plurals by changing *y* to *i* and adding *es*. One plural is not a noun plural. [pp. 33-34]

It would seem probable that most children who are old enough to need to spell the first eight exceptions should be sufficiently familiar with the pronunciation to guard against any great amount of interference from plurals in *s* or *es*. *Leaves* and *lives* as well as plurals ending in *ies* are undoubtedly misspelled many times. Probably these are phonetic misspellings that would occur anyway.

Since it has been estimated that this rule of plurals could be simply taught in not more than four lessons, it seems fair to suppose that, if the rule were understood and applied by grade school children, the time would be profitably spent.

Perhaps attention should be called to the second part of the rule which says "*Es* is added to make the word easier to pronounce." This was substituted for the usual naming of letters which are followed by *es*, in an attempt to simplify the rule. It was recognized that plurals ending in *sts* would cause trouble. Since there was only one such plural, the word *lists* in Grade 8, this danger was not considered serious.

It would seem probable that children in the grades actually use more than one such plural. Surely many *ghostes* appear each year at Hallowe'en. Certainly such words are easier to pronounce with *es* added instead of *s*.

In an attempt to see what would happen if plurals ending in *sts* were included in a spelling list, seven of such plurals were placed in the pre-tests. Table 2 shows the results. Only those words that were misspelled in the *sts* part of the word were counted wrong.

The number of children spelling each word was about 70 each for Grades 3, 4, 5, and 6; 30 for Grade 7; and 55 for Grade 8.

It will be observed that even in the eighth grade some of the less familiar words are misspelled by as high as 33 and 49 per cent.

Table 1 shows that Rule II has a frequency of 167 with only 4 exceptions. These words occur in Grades 2 to 8 inclusive.

TABLE 2

PERCENTAGE OF ERRORS IN SPELLING *sts* PLURALS

WORD	GRADE					
	3*	4	5	6	7	8
1. Wrists	82	62	57	29	23	9
2. Frosts	83	54	40	40	32	16
3. Fists	68	58	31	30	29	5
4. Ghosts	74	50	43	53		13
5. Lists				25	10	17
6. Crusts				39		33
7. Interests				48		49

* Eighty-two per cent of the children in Grade 3 who spelled *wrists* misspelled the *sts* part.

Since this rule also could probably be taught in three or four lessons, it would prove very profitable if children could learn to use it.

Rule III has 56 words spread throughout Grades 3 to 8 with one exception.

Rule IV governs 54 words in Grades 4 to 8 with no exceptions. It has been estimated that this rule could be taught in two lessons.

The case for Rule V is not so clear. There are 101 words having *ie* and 30 words having *ei*. In thirteen of these words *ei* has the sound of long ā. *Ie* has 9 exceptions and *ei* has 8 exceptions.[1] Sartorius says: "Counting the thirteen words that sound like ā and thinking only in terms of visual appearance, there are thirty words out of 131 that do not conform to the rule." [13, p. 39]

If the spelling of words that relate to Rule V were controlled by visual appearance the phrase "Or when sounded as ā as in *neighbor* and *weigh*" would prove useless. These words would then need to be added to the exceptions and there would be about one-third as many exceptions as words following the rule.

Although the value of this rule seemed very doubtful, it was decided to test it in order to see what would really happen. Since the interchanging of *ie* and *ei* is one of the fifteen most common types of errors given by Sartorius any device for determining the correct order would be very helpful. [13, p. 52]

[1] Exceptions to *ie* are being, seeing, either, neither, foreign, height, seize, foreigner, and leisure.
Exceptions to *ei* are society, science, vacancies, ancient, conscience, efficiency, efficient, and conscientious.

Rule VI, not given by Sartorius, governs 330 words in Grades 2 to 8 and has 20 exceptions. Since the substitution of *i* or *ey* for final *y* is one of these same fifteen most common errors, it would seem that this rule should prove very profitable.

Rule VII is long and involved. Moreover, there are only 45 words with 13 exceptions. It is easy to agree with Sartorius when she says: "The rule seems more confusing than helpful. It may be harder to learn the rule and its exceptions than to learn to spell the words separately." [p. 38] It was decided to try this rule also to see how difficult it would be to learn and to apply.

CHAPTER IV

TEACHING THE RULES

Children in Experiment

This experiment was conducted in a public school on Long Island during March and April, 1931. Three classes were selected from each grade on the basis of the general intelligence of the children, as measured by standard tests.

When available, a Stanford-Binet intelligence quotient was used to determine the mental age at the beginning of the experiment. All other mental ages were determined by a group test given during the experiment. The National Intelligence Test, Form A, was given in Grades 4, 5, and 6, and the Terman Group Test of Mental Ability, in Grades 7 and 8.

All the children in the grade sections chosen were taught the lessons and took the final examinations. In tabulating the results by grades the experimenter used only the papers of those children whose intelligence quotients ranged between 90 and 110. In tabulating the results by mental ages all papers were included except those of children who had been absent for some part of the lessons on a spelling rule.

Teachers of Lessons

In this experiment no attempt was made to equalize teaching ability. Since all the teachers who participated were well above average both in training and in experience, it was felt that they would teach equally well the simple plans that were used in these lessons.

That this was true in the main was shown by the distribution of scores in the final examinations. It was found that when the scores of one section of a grade were consistently lower than those of other sections, an examination of errors showed that some part of the work had been neglected. This was particularly true, in the case of the statement of the rule. Occasionally a teacher had failed to learn the rule with care and an entire class wrote a much abbreviated statement. However, these slight deficiencies might occur within any group of teachers. The tabulations gave some indication that teachers who were accustomed to teaching the slower children gave more careful drill on the work covered.

Teaching Preliminary Terms

Since the purpose of this study was to determine the children's ability to understand and to apply the ideas expressed in the rules, it seemed necessary to have a preliminary study of all unfamiliar terms used in stating the rules. Accordingly, the following terms were selected:

1. Noun
2. Singular
3. Plural
4. Vowel
5. Consonant
6. Double letter
7. Syllable
8. Accented syllable
9. Suffix
10. Final letter
11. Preceded by
12. Short sounds of *e* and *i*
13. Letters of the alphabet

When the test on the above list was given, it was found that all the terms had been well learned except the short sounds of *i* and *e*, and the placing of the accent in a word. It was therefore necessary to supply this information in the tests.

In the test on Rule VI the examination stated that all the words to be respelled ended in some sound of *i*. In the examination on Rule VII the accent was marked on all spelling words.

Pre-Tests on Words

The grade pre-tests on each rule were made up of the words governed by the rule occurring in that grade plus those found in the two grades above. For Grades 7 and 8, extra words were taken from Horn's *A Basic Writing Vocabulary* [7] and from Ashbaugh's *The Iowa Spelling Scales* [2].

In scoring, only those words that were misspelled in the part covered by the rule were counted wrong. After the words were scored tabulations were made of the frequency of misspellings of each word to see whether all grades needed to study a given rule, and to obtain, also, word lists which could be used for drilling and testing the rules.

GRADE DISTRIBUTION OF RULES

The grades in which each rule was taught were determined by the frequency of misspellings by grades of the words governed by the rule, and by the frequency of occurrence by grades of these words. Table 3 gives this distribution and also the number of lessons given for each rule.

TABLE 3
SHOWING GRADE DISTRIBUTION AND NUMBER OF LESSONS FOR EACH RULE

RULE	GRADE	NUMBER OF LESSONS
I	3–8	3
II	3–8	3
III	5–8	3
IV	4–8	2
V	5–8	3
VI	3–7	3
VII	5–8	5

Rules III, IV, and V were left out of some of the lower grades because there were not sufficient words governed by the rule to justify teaching them. Rule VI was not taught in Grade 8 because so few children missed words ending in *y* that the rule seemed unnecessary. Rule VII was so involved that it seemed useless to try to teach it below Grade 5.

LESSON PLANS

A series of lessons was planned for each rule and tried out by the experimenter. After these had been revised and mimeographed they were given to each teacher.

An attempt was made to control the amount of drill by stating the number of times the rules should be repeated, and by supplying uniform drill materials. There was also an attempt to control the discussion by stating how many children should respond to a given question before the teacher should give the correct answer.

The lessons were planned for a fifteen-minute period, but twenty minutes were allowed when necessary. In the examinations the upper grades usually finished in less than fifteen minutes. It may be that, if the upper grade pupils had made a more thoughtful application of some of the rules, the exercises would have taken longer and the results would have been better.

Examinations on Rules

Each examination on a rule contained three sections. Section I asked for a statement of the rule. Section II called for the spelling of words taken from the Gates-Graham list, Horn's *A Basic Writing Vocabulary*, and *The Iowa Spelling Scales*. These were called *real* words. Section III required the spelling of non-sense words according to the rule. In both Sections II and III the words were mimeographed as a part of the examination so that they were presented visually to the children.

The rules taught called for two kinds of responses in spelling words: one was adding suffixes to root words; the other was making an internal change in a word. For the first kind the root word and the suffix were given and the children wrote the deriva-tives. For the second, words were misspelled in various ways. For Rule IV the *u* following *q* was omitted. In Rule V the *i* and *e* were interchanged. In Rule VI final *y* was misspelled by sub-stituting *e, ie,* or *ey*.

In order that the children might not spell the words in a routine manner, some root words and some suffixes that did not follow the rule were included. Also, among the words requiring internal changes some correct spellings were included.

Nonsense Words

Since the same examination was given to all grades, it was necessary to do something to overcome the effect of the superior knowledge of words possessed by the upper grades. Another obstacle presented itself in the fact that difficulty lists of spelling words now available are based on the difficulty of the words as a whole, and therefore not suitable for the purpose of this investi-gation. The pre-tests showed that the difficulty of the whole word was not the difficulty of the part governed by the rule.

As one way of overcoming this difficulty words equally unknown to all were used. Nonsense words were selected for the purpose.

Scoring the Examination

Each rule was separated into main ideas and one point was given for each idea. Reference to the tables giving the distribu-tion of scores on the statement of the rule will give the number of points for each rule.

The words spelled were each scored one. A word was counted wrong only if misspelled in the part governed by the rule or so closely associated with it as to seem caused by some change made necessary by the rule.

To illustrate: a part of the test on Rule IV was the respelling of words, most of which had omitted the *u* following the *q*. If a child followed the *q* by *u* but dropped the vowel that should have followed *u*, the word was counted wrong. It seemed probable that the child thought that the *u* should be substituted for the letter following *q*.

After the examinations were corrected the tabulations mentioned in Chapter II were made and the results were interpreted for each rule.

CHAPTER V

INTERPRETATION OF RESULTS OF FINAL EXAMINATIONS ON RULES

TREATMENT OF DATA

The scores obtained on the final examinations were tabulated by grades and by mental ages. Similar distributions were made for scores obtained on the three sections of the examination. The percentage of each grade and of each mental age obtaining a given score was found for each rule, after which a classification of errors by grades was made for each section of the examination. Finally all the data for each rule were studied in an effort to find significant ideas for teaching these rules. In interpreting the data some of the most significant facts were found, not in the scores on the examinations, but in the study of errors.

Table 4 gives the distribution of mental ages by grades. In general it was found that the distribution of scores by mental

TABLE 4

DISTRIBUTION BY GRADES OF MENTAL AGE OF CHILDREN

MENTAL AGE	GRADE					
	3	4	5	6	7	8
16						2
15					4	12
14				2	13	17
13				10	12	5
12			5	21	5	
11		9	22	10	2	
10	8	23	11	2		
9	37	15	1			
8	19	1				
7	2					
Average	8.8	9.8	10.8	12.0	13.3	14.3

NOTE: The mental age was reckoned by taking that of the nearest year; that is, a mental age of 9 years ranged from 8 years 7 months to 9 years 6 months.

ages agreed with the distribution of the grade having the same average mental age.

INTERPRETATION OF DATA FOR RULE I

Rule—Most nouns form their plurals by adding s or es to the singular. Es is added to make the word easier to pronounce. (See Tables 5–12.)

Table 5 shows that the scores on the examination as a whole gradually increase from grade to grade. A few pupils in Grades 6, 7, and 8, and one in Grade 3, received perfect scores.

In the distribution of scores for the three parts of the rule as shown in Tables 6, 7, and 8, it is seen that Grades 5 to 8 did better than Grades 3 and 4.

It seemed to the author that the data did not justify any refined statistical treatment; therefore, in general the figures are quoted

TABLE 5

Rule I—Plurals in s and es

DISTRIBUTION BY GRADES OF PERCENTAGE OF CHILDREN RECEIVING EACH SCORE ON THE EXAMINATION AS A WHOLE

SCORE	GRADE					
	3	4	5	6	7	8
27	2			17	9	23
26			14	6	15	6
25	4	7	6	3	18	17
24	7	5	3	14	18	14
23	7	7	11	17	6	17
22	9	10	9	3	9	11
21	9	12	6	20	12	
20	9	12	11	6	6	
19	9	12	9	6		
18	7	5	6			9
17			3	6	3	
16	4	10	9		3	
15	7	10	3	3		3
14	7	5	9			
13	11	5	3			
12	2					
11	4					
0						
N per Grade* . . .	54	41	35	35	33	35

*In all tables throughout this study *N* represents Number of Cases.

TABLE 6

Rule I—Plurals in s and es

DISTRIBUTION BY GRADES OF PERCENTAGE OF CHILDREN RECEIVING EACH
SCORE ON THE STATEMENT OF THE RULE

SCORE	GRADE					
	3	4	5	6	7	8
9	13		11	37	36	43
8	15		17	6	21	23
7	20	19	8	6	6	9
6	6	19	6	14	6	6
5	9	27	14	23	12	9
4		2	6	3	15	3
3	9	10	11	6	3	3
2		5	6	3		3
1						
0	28	17	20	3		3
N per Grade . . .	54	41	35	35	33	35

TABLE 7

Rule I—Plurals in s and es

DISTRIBUTION BY GRADES OF PERCENTAGE OF CHILDREN RECEIVING EACH
SCORE ON SPELLING REAL WORDS

SCORE	GRADE					
	3	4	5	6	7	8
9	22	44	37	63	73	74
8	15	27	34	14	21	17
7	44	27	26	20	6	9
6	17		3	3		
5						
4	2	2				
3						
2						
1						
0						
N per Grade	54	41	35	35	33	35

TABLE 8

Rule I—Plurals in s and es

<small>DISTRIBUTION BY GRADES OF PERCENTAGE OF CHILDREN RECEIVING EACH
SCORE ON SPELLING NONSENSE WORDS</small>

SCORE	GRADE					
	3	4	5	6	7	8
9	9	15	26	40	39	40
8	11	20	29	26	18	26
7	15	17	20	9	30	11
6	52	46	26	23	6	23
5	6	2		3	3	
4	6					
3	2				3	
2						
1						
0						
N per Grade	54	41	35	35	33	35

to show what proportion of the children received certain scores.
Table 6 shows that in Grade 3, 13 per cent of the children made
perfect scores on the statement of the rule and 15 per cent missed
only one point. Combining these two per cents we find that 28
per cent of all the children in Grade 3 missed one point or less
in the statement of Rule I. A similar statement that would cover
the achievement of all grades would read: The percentage of each
grade missing one point or less (out of a total of nine points)
on the statement of the rule is 28 for Grade 3, 0 for Grade 4,
28 for Grade 5, 43 for Grade 6, 57 for Grade 7, and 66 for
Grade 8. In all groups except the fourth there are some zero
scores and some perfect. It would seem that these results could
fairly be interpreted as indicating an unsatisfactory grasp of the
statement of the rule.

After the examination some of the teachers said that they had
taught the two parts of the rule as two separate rules. The tabulation of errors showed that this was probably true in several
cases. Thirty-eight per cent of all children in all grades who
wrote the rule missed the second part. This proportion is also
fairly consistent for each grade. Another common error was the
omission of *most*; this error occurred 43 per cent of the time in
the rules written.

TABLE 9

Rule I—Plurals in s and es

DISTRIBUTION BY MENTAL AGES OF PERCENTAGE OF CHILDREN RECEIVING EACH SCORE ON THE EXAMINATION AS A WHOLE

SCORE	MENTAL AGE							
	8	9	10	11	12	13	14	15
27		2	2	6	10	6	17	20
26		2	2	8		10	8	20
25		3	5	6	8	6	21	16
24	4	10	10	12	14	16	17	8
23	4	5	10	6	16	8	8	8
22	4	12	10	10	4	10	8	8
21	11	12	10	15	16	10	6	4
20	11	7	8	6	12	6	6	
19	11	8	5	10	8		2	
18	7	7	10	4	2	8	4	8
17			7	8	4	10		
16		8	5	2	2	2		4
15	11	5	12	6	2	2		4
14	11	3	3	2	2	2		
13	11	12	2	2	2	2		
12	7	2						
11	7	3						
0								
N per Age	27	60	60	52	51	49	48	25

In the spelling of real words the percentage of each grade missing one word or less out of a total of nine was 57 for Grade 3, 71 for Grades 4 and 5, 77 for Grade 6, 94 for Grade 7, and 91 for Grade 8. The high scores in Grades 7 and 8 are probably due to previous knowledge of the words.

In spelling nonsense words these high scores were not maintained. Here the percentage of children missing one word or less out of a total of nine words was 21 for Grade 3, 35 for Grade 4, 55 for Grade 5, 66 for Grade 6, 57 for Grade 7, and 66 for Grade 8.

The study of errors showed that the confusion which existed in regard to adding *es* when stating the rule carried over to spelling. Many children added *es* when the letters were necessary to make all words end in *es*. A few added *es* when only *s* was needed to give an extra syllable. The percentage of the possible number of

TABLE 10

Rule I—Plurals in s and es

DISTRIBUTION BY MENTAL AGES OF PERCENTAGE OF CHILDREN RECEIVING EACH SCORE ON THE STATEMENT OF THE RULE

SCORE	MENTAL AGE							
	8	9	10	11	12	13	14	15
9	11	7	8	17	27	16	38	36
8	4	15	3	21	5	18	25	20
7	7	20	25	10	8	12	2	12
6	7	8	13	13	24	12	13	8
5	4	12	13	15	22	10	8	4
4	4			6	4	6	6	12
3	15	12	7	6	4	2	6	4
2	4	2	12	2	2	2		
1		2	2					
0	44	23	17	10	6	20	2	4
N per Age	27	60	60	52	51	49	48	25

TABLE 11

Rule I—Plurals in s and es

DISTRIBUTION BY MENTAL AGES OF PERCENTAGE OF CHILDREN RECEIVING EACH SCORE ON SPELLING REAL WORDS

SCORE	MENTAL AGE							
	8	9	10	11	12	13	14	15
9	19	27	37	42	43	65	67	88
8	11	20	30	19	29	18	23	4
7	44	43	22	33	25	16	8	8
6	22	10	8	6	2			
5			2					
4	4		2				2	
3								
2								
1								
0								
N per Age	27	60	60	52	51	49	48	25

TABLE 12

Rule I—Plurals in s and es

DISTRIBUTION BY MENTAL AGES OF PERCENTAGE OF CHILDREN RECEIVING
EACH SCORE ON SPELLING NONSENSE WORDS

SCORE	MENTAL AGE							
	8	9	10	11	12	13	14	15
9	7	12	20	27	29	33	54	56
8	15	17	30	23	20	31	21	12
7	15	13	17	19	18	20	13	8
6	41	53	28	27	29	12	13	20
5	19	2	3	4	2	2		
4	4	2	2		2	2		
3		2						4
2								
1								
0								
N per Age	27	60	60	52	51	49	48	25

es errors made by each grade in spelling real words was 57 for
Grade 3, 37 for Grade 4, 38 for Grade 5, 23 for Grade 6, 8 for
Grade 7, and 14 for Grade 8. This error accounted for 71 per
cent of all errors in Grade 3, 79 in Grade 4, 88 in Grade 5, 70 in
Grade 6, 58 in Grade 7, and 83 in Grade 8.

The spelling of nonsense words gave more *es* errors. The percentage of possible number of errors made was 76 for Grade 3,
61 for Grade 4, 49 for Grade 5, 27 for Grade 6, 34 for Grade 7,
and 36 for Grade 8. When compared with all other errors made
in spelling these nonsense words, the percentage of *es* errors was
found to be 85 for Grade 3, 87 for Grade 4, 95 for Grade 5, 84
for Grade 6, 87 for Grade 7, and 95 for Grade 8. It will thus
be seen that not only did the grades make a high percentage of
possible errors in adding *es* to words but also that these errors
were the only ones that occurred at all frequently.

During the time devoted to the rule on plurals, adding *s* and *es*
were taught on consecutive days. No doubt less confusion would
occur if the two parts of the rule were separated by an interval
of several weeks. Moreover, since the Gates-Graham list contains only eight plurals that require the addition of *es*, it might
prove more profitable to teach them without reference to any rule.
This elimination of the second part of the rule would probably

make it possible to teach adding *s* for plurals in the second half of Grade 3 or at least in Grade 4.

It may be that in everyday spelling the difficulty with this rule would prove to be largely one of grammar. Undoubtedly children in the lower grades would have trouble distinguishing nouns from other parts of speech. In the final examination on plurals this ability was not tested, but the examination on preliminary terms showed a lack of clear understanding of the term *noun*. Moreover, the rule as formulated omits the large class of words that are not nouns in which the addition of *s* and *es* comes up as, for instance, *sit, sits; burst, bursts; push, pushes;* and *teach, teaches.*

It might prove more profitable to omit all ideas from grammar and to make the adding of *s* and *es* dependent on phonic generalization. If this were done, probably no rule would be taught; but, when necessary, attention would be called to the phonic spelling. Ability to spell would then depend on mental pronunciation. Probably children who would need to spell these words should have learned their pronunciation.

The distribution of scores by mental ages showed about the same conditions as were present in grades having the same mental ages for an average.

Interpretation of Data for Rule II

Rule—Drop the final e before adding a suffix beginning with a vowel. (See Tables 13–20.)

For Rule II there is a general tendency for the scores to increase from grade to grade. Grades 5 to 8 did considerably better than Grades 3 and 4. Many perfect scores were made in the higher grades. In Grades 6 and 7 at least 97 per cent of the children missed only one point or less out of a perfect score of 23. The percentage for Grade 8 was considerably lowered because in one section half the class did not write the rule. In a second section everyone received a perfect score and in the third, all except one pupil did equally well.

The separate tabulations for the three parts of the examination show a fairly even increase of percentages receiving higher scores, except for the statement of the rule in Grade 8 and except for the lower maximum in the scores for all parts in Grade 4. In one section of Grade 4 more than half the class left out the phrase "beginning with a vowel."

TABLE 13

Rule II—Dropping Final e

DISTRIBUTION BY GRADES OF PERCENTAGE OF CHILDREN RECEIVING EACH
SCORE ON THE EXAMINATION AS A WHOLE

SCORE	GRADE					
	3	4	5	6	7	8
23	41	17	58	87	81	63
22	5	26	17	10	16	9
21	13	12	6			6
20	5	7	8			17
19	5	7	8			3
18	7	5	3			
17	2	2				
16	4					
15	2	2				
14		5				3
13		5		3		
12	2	2				
11	7	5				
10	5	2				
9	2					
8		2				
0						
N per Grade	56	42	36	39	31	35

TABLE 14

Rule II—Dropping Final e

DISTRIBUTION BY GRADES OF PERCENTAGE OF CHILDREN RECEIVING EACH
SCORE ON THE STATEMENT OF THE RULE

SCORE	GRADE					
	3	4	5	6	7	8
3	52	50	75	100	94	66
2	13	24	3		6	9
1	11	17	3			6
0	25	19	19			20
N per Grade	56	42	36	39	31	35

TABLE 15

Rule II—Dropping Final e

DISTRIBUTION BY GRADES OF PERCENTAGE OF CHILDREN RECEIVING EACH
SCORE ON SPELLING REAL WORDS

SCORE	GRADE					
	3	4	5	6	7	8
10	71	67	86	95	94	100
9	7	21	14	5	3	
8	7	5				
7		2			3	
6	9	2				
5	2	2				
4	2					
3	2					
2						
1						
0						
N per Grade	56	42	36	39	31	35

TABLE 16

Rule II—Dropping Final e

DISTRIBUTION BY GRADES OF PERCENTAGE OF CHILDREN RECEIVING EACH
SCORE ON SPELLING NONSENSE WORDS

SCORE	GRADE					
	3	4	5	6	7	8
10	59	43	83	92	90	91
9	9	12	14	5	10	6
8	11	19	3			
7		2				
6	2	2				
5	11	2				
4	5	2				
3	2	2				
2		2				3
1		5				
0	2	7				
N per Grade	56	42	36	39	31	35

TABLE 17

Rule II—Dropping Final e

DISTRIBUTION BY MENTAL AGES OF PERCENTAGE OF CHILDREN RECEIVING
EACH SCORE ON THE EXAMINATION AS A WHOLE

SCORE	MENTAL AGE							
	8	9	10	11	12	13	14	15
23	25	36	39	60	58	74	76	75
22	13	11	16	15	25	15	7	13
21	17	11	11	7	8	4	4	
20	8	13	5	6	2	4	9	8
19	4	5	5	7	2	2	4	
18	8	5	5		2			
17		3	3			2		
16		2	2					
15		2	3					
14			2	2				4
13	8		2		2			
12	4	2	2					
11	4	5	3					
10	4	5		2	2			
9	4							
8			2					
7								
6								
5								
4								
3			2					
2								
1								
0								
N per Age	24	61	62	53	53	53	46	24

A comparison of the scores obtained in spelling the real words
and the nonsense words shows that the percentages for each grade
run somewhat lower for the nonsense words. The grades hold
about the same relative position in both scores.

The scores on the nonsense words were usually lower. This
was to be expected because of the unfamiliarity of the material.
Thorndike made a study on "The Effect of Changed Data upon
Reasoning" [15] in which he concluded that:

On the whole, it seems certain that even such slight changes as
from the customary a, b, x and y, to k and p or p_1, p_2 and p_3 or to p_1, p_{11}, p_{111},
impede thought, and that the general theorem does hold that "Any dis-

turbance whatsoever in the concrete particulars reasoned about will interfere with reasoning." [p. 38]

If this statement is true, we should expect the scores on nonsense words to run lower than on real words even if the spelling of both were equally unlearned before a study of the rule.

Occasionally some of the nonsense words scored higher. This seemed to be due to the interference of known words in the

TABLE 18

Rule II—Dropping Final e

DISTRIBUTION BY MENTAL AGES OF PERCENTAGE OF CHILDREN RECEIVING EACH SCORE ON THE STATEMENT OF THE RULE

SCORE	MENTAL AGE							
	8	9	10	11	12	13	14	15
3	42	48	61	83	79	81	83	75
2	25	16	16	8	9	11		17
1	8	12	5		6	2	7	
0	25	25	18	9	6	6	11	8
N per Age	24	61	62	53	53	53	46	24

TABLE 19

Rule II—Dropping Final e

DISTRIBUTION BY MENTAL AGES OF PERCENTAGE OF CHILDREN RECEIVING EACH SCORE ON SPELLING REAL WORDS

SCORE	MENTAL AGE							
	8	9	10	11	12	13	14	15
10	63	74	76	89	87	92	98	100
9	17	10	18	9	13	8		
8	8	7		2				
7		2					2	
6	4	7	3					
5	4		2					
4	4							
3		2	2					
2								
1								
0								
N per Age	24	61	62	53	53	53	46	24

TABLE 20

Rule II—Dropping Final e

DISTRIBUTION BY MENTAL AGES OF PERCENTAGE OF CHILDREN RECEIVING
EACH SCORE ON SPELLING NONSENSE WORDS

SCORE	MENTAL AGE							
	8	9	10	11	12	13	14	15
10	54	59	58	74	89	89	91	96
9	8	18	15	11	6	8	9	
8	13	10	5	9		4		
7			2	2				
6			5					
5	13	5	2		2			
4		5	5					
3			3					
2	4		2					4
1	4		2	4				
0	4	3	3		4			
N per Age	24	61	62	53	53	53	46	24

spelling of real words. Archer [1] made a study in which he found that, if root words were learned first, they interfered with the spelling of derivatives requiring a change in the root word, while if derivatives were learned first, they interfered with the spelling of root words.

Further tabulation in the present study showed that 11 per cent of all children failed to write any part of Rule II. This failure constituted about one-third of all errors made. Fourteen per cent omitted the phrase "beginning with a vowel." These two omissions made up 40 per cent of all errors made in the test.

In spelling the real words 31 per cent of all errors were due to omissions either of the suffix or of the entire word. Forty-three per cent of the errors consisted in not dropping the *e* before adding the suffix *ing*. Four per cent of the possible number of errors in adding *ing* were made by the grades as a whole. In Grades 3 and 4, 22 per cent made errors of the *ing* type. In all grades the total of these errors in adding *ing* was 39. Thirty-eight of these were in Grades 3 and 4.

Although there were as many chances to add the suffix *ed* as that of *ing*, there was only one case in which final *e* was not dropped. The suffix *er* occurred half as many times as that of *ing* or *ed* but was incorrectly added only once. So far as adding suffixes is concerned, it would seem that *ing* is the only one that requires much emphasis. It may be that the pupils' successful dropping of final *e* when adding *er* and *ed* is due more to the appearance of the word than to the application of the rule. Possibly the two *e*'s that result from not dropping the final *e* do not look right to the children.

In spelling nonsense words 37 per cent of all errors were omissions; 13 per cent consisted in changing the nonsense words to real words. These changes occurred in Grades 4 and 6 and were found in only a few papers. Again the largest number of errors occurred in failing to drop the final *e* when adding the suffix *ing*. This error occurred 68 times, 60 of which were in Grades 3 and 4. The chances of making this error in the nonsense words as compared with similar chances in the real words were as 5 to 4. However, it is easily seen that even in proportion the errors occurred more times in the nonsense words. Very few errors were made in failure to drop final *e* before adding *ed* or *er*.

In regard to teaching Rule II in Grades 3 to 8, the conclusion seems justified that if emphasis is placed on adding the suffix *ing* in Grades 3 and 4 the children will be able to understand and to apply it when their minds are centered on the task. Since the Gates-Graham list gives only six *ing* words in Grade 3, and seven in Grade 4, it may prove more profitable to teach these words independent of the rule and to use them as the basis for introducing the rule in Grade 5.

An examination of the distribution of scores by mental ages showed that the facts for ages 8, 9, and 10 were similar to those for Grades 3 and 4. At the time of this experiment the average mental age of Grade 3 was approximately 9 years and for Grade 4, 10 years. Since the facts for these mental ages and for the grades are in such close agreement, it seems reasonable to assume that, if a distribution of errors for Rule II were made by mental ages, we would find very nearly the same results for ages 8, 9, and 10 as were found for Grades 3 and 4.

INTERPRETATION OF DATA FOR RULE III

When final y is preceded by a consonant, change the y to i before adding any suffix that does not begin with i. (See Tables 21–28.)

TABLE 21

Rule III—Changing y to i

DISTRIBUTION BY GRADES OF PERCENTAGE OF CHILDREN RECEIVING EACH
SCORE ON THE EXAMINATION AS A WHOLE

SCORE	GRADE			
	5	6	7	8
26	3	13	29	25
25	3	8	16	16
24	11	11	23	16
23	9	18	10	3
22	11	21	6	13
21	14	3	3	3
20	3	3	3	
19		3		3
18	14	3	3	
17	3			
16	6	3	3	6
15		3		6
14	3			
13	6			3
12	3			3
11	3	5		
10	3	3		3
9				
8				
7		3		
6	3			
5			3	
4				
3				
2		3		
1				
0				
N per Grade	35	38	31	32

The distribution of scores by grades for the examination as a
whole showed that Grades 6, 7, and 8 learned the rule better than
Grade 5. The percentage of each grade missing one point or
less out of a perfect score of 26 was 5 for Grade 5, 21 for Grade 6,
45 for Grade 7, and 41 for Grade 8.

The distribution of scores by grade sections for the three parts
of the examination showed that in the statement of the rule one
fifth, one sixth, and one eighth grade were below the other two
sections of the respective grades. The tabulation of errors

TABLE 22

Rule III—Changing y to i

DISTRIBUTION BY GRADES OF PERCENTAGE OF CHILDREN RECEIVING EACH
SCORE ON THE STATEMENT OF THE RULE

SCORE	GRADE			
	5	6	7	8
4	14	47	81	44
3	20	39	10	34
2	14		6	9
1	20	5	3	6
0	31	8		6
N per Grade	35	38	31	32

TABLE 23

Rule III—Changing y to i

DISTRIBUTION BY GRADES OF PERCENTAGE OF CHILDREN RECEIVING EACH
SCORE ON SPELLING REAL WORDS

SCORE	GRADE			
	5	6	7	8
11	14	50	48	53
10	40	21	29	19
9	14	11	10	22
8	9	5	6	3
7	9		3	3
6	6			
5		5		
4		3		
3	3			
2				
1		3	3	
0	3	3		
N per Grade	35	38	31	32

showed that this entire fifth grade omitted the phrase "before adding any suffix that does not begin with *i*." This part of the rule was
evidently not taught. In the sixth grade with the low score all but
one pupil missed this phrase and in the eighth grade section approximately half the class made the same mistake. Since most of
the other grades also missed this part of the rule more than any

TABLE 24

Rule III—Changing y to i

DISTRIBUTION BY GRADES OF PERCENTAGE OF CHILDREN RECEIVING EACH SCORE ON SPELLING NONSENSE WORDS

SCORE	GRADE			
	5	6	7	8
11	26	26	55	41
10	23	32	16	38
9	14	13	13	
8	11		3	
7	6	11	6	
6			3	3
5	6			9
4	3			3
3	3	8		
2	6	5		
1		5	3	6
0	3			
N per Grade	35	38	31	32

other, it probably was difficult to remember. In fact this one error accounted for 45 per cent of all those made in the statement of the rule.

In Part II of the examination, the spelling of real words, almost exactly half the children in Grades 6, 7, and 8 had perfect scores. In Grade 5 only 14 per cent had scores equally high. However, part of the ability to spell these real words was probably due to previous knowledge.

In spelling the nonsense words Grades 5 and 6 each had 26 per cent with perfect scores. The percentages of those in Grades 5 to 8 who missed one word or less were 49, 58, 71, and 79 respectively. There was considerable scattering for all grades.

The study of errors for the real words showed that 43 per cent of all errors was dropping the final *y*. Since there were 11 chances to drop final *y* in each paper and 155 children took the test, this error was made only 7 per cent of the possible number of times. Also the fact that this error was found in only a few papers makes it even less important. Probably there was some interference from Rule II, dropping final *e*, which was taught just preceding this rule.

TABLE 25

Rule III—Changing y to

DISTRIBUTION BY MENTAL AGES OF PERCENTAGE OF CHILDREN RECEIVING EACH SCORE ON THE EXAMINATION AS A WHOLE

SCORE	MENTAL AGE					
	10	11	12	13	14	15
26	6	6	11	2	27	53
25	6	6	14	8	13	33
24	6	14	14	28	16	13
23	6	19	11	6	7	7
22		14	19	18	13	13
21	19	6	3	4	4	
20		3	8		4	
19				12		13
18	19	3	5		4	
17		3		2	2	
16		8	5		2	13
15			3		2	7
14		3	3			
13		3	3			
12	6					7
11	6		3	2		
10		6		4	2	
9				2		
8						
7		3				
6	6					
5					2	
4						
3	6					
2		3				
1						
0	13	3				
N per Age	16	36	37	50	45	24

Not changing the *y* to *i* accounted for 29 per cent of all errors. Since there were 9 chances to make this error on each paper, 6 per cent of the possible number of errors was made. This error also tended to be constant and was found in only a few papers.

Another error, that of changing *y* to *i* when *y* was not preceded by a consonant, seems more important. This accounted for 18 per cent of all errors. Since there was only one chance to make this mistake on each paper, it was made 30 per cent of the possible number. This error is also important for its spread through-

TABLE 26

Rule III—Changing y to i

DISTRIBUTION BY MENTAL AGES OF PERCENTAGE OF CHILDREN RECEIVING
EACH SCORE ON THE STATEMENT OF THE RULE

SCORE	MENTAL AGE						
	9	10	11	12	13	14	15
4	50	19	33	49	32	49	75
3	17	13	28	28	48	36	8
2	17	6	11	5	8	4	8
1		25	14	3	4	2	4
0	17	38	14	14	8	9	4
N per Age	6	16	36	37	50	45	24

TABLE 27

Rule III—Changing y to i

DISTRIBUTION BY MENTAL AGES OF PERCENTAGE OF CHILDREN RECEIVING
EACH SCORE ON SPELLING REAL WORDS

SCORE	MENTAL AGE						
	9	10	11	12	13	14	15
11	17	19	22	35	30	49	50
10	33	19	28	38	30	20	33
9	50	19	14	16	24	20	8
8			11	5	8	4	4
7		13	6		2	2	4
6		6	6	3	2		
5					2	2	
4			3	3	2		
3				3			
2		6					
1		6	3			2	
0		13	6				
N per Age	6	16	36	37	50	45	24

out the grades. It occurred 40 per cent of the possible number
of times in Grade 5, 29 in Grades 6 and 7, and 17 in Grade 8.
Probably the greatest significance of this error lies in its indication of a lack of thoughtful application of the rule. Evidently
many children were indiscriminately changing *y* to *i*.

TABLE 28

Rule III—Changing y to i

DISTRIBUTION BY MENTAL AGES OF PERCENTAGE OF CHILDREN RECEIVING
EACH SCORE ON SPELLING NONSENSE WORDS

SCORE	MENTAL AGE						
	9	10	11	12	13	14	15
11	17	25	19	32	40	47	54
10	50	19	31	32	34	31	17
9	17	13	19	5	8	2	13
8	17	6	6	3	6	7	
7			6	8	4	4	4
6				3			4
5		6	6	5	2	4	4
4				3			
3		6	3	3	4		
2		6	6	3			
1			3			4	4
0		19	3	3	2		
N per Age	6	16	36	37	50	45	24

The errors in nonsense words were similar to those in real words. Final *y* was dropped 8 per cent of the possible number of times. *Y* was not changed to *i* 9 per cent of the possible number. The changing of final *y* to *i* when it was not preceded by a consonant dropped from 30 per cent of the possible number to 12. All except one of these errors occurred in Grades 5 and 6. It may be that the greater thoughtfulness made necessary by the unfamiliar nonsense words caused this change.

The distribution of scores by mental ages showed a general tendency toward an increase with mental age. At a mental age of 11 years 6 per cent of the children received perfect scores. At mental age 15, 33 per cent had perfect scores. There also tended to be a decrease in the scatter of the scores. Mental age 11 had a scatter from a perfect score of 26 to 0. Mental age 15 ranged from perfect through 12. The distribution of scores by sections showed the same general trend.

It would seem that children in Grades 5 to 8 should be able to use this rule, if emphasis is placed on *not* changing final *y* to *i* when it is not preceded by a consonant. Special attention should be given to those words to which this caution applies.

INTERPRETATION OF DATA FOR RULE IV

Rule—Q is always followed by u. (See Tables 29–36.)

The scores for this rule were generally high for all grades with very little scatter. The percentage of children missing one point or less on the examination as a whole was 63 for Grade 4, 80 for Grade 5, 93 for Grade 6, 91 for Grade 7, and 88 for Grade 8.

This high scoring obtained throughout the three sections of the test. The percentage receiving a perfect score on the rule was 84 for Grade 4, 92 for Grade 5, 95 for Grade 6, 100 for Grade 7, and 91 for Grade 8.

The percentage of children missing one word or less of the real words was 95 for Grade 4, 97 for Grade 5, and 100 for Grades 6, 7, and 8. On the whole the nonsense words were spelled somewhat less accurately. The percentage missing one word or less was 83 for Grade 4, 94 for Grade 5, 100 for Grade 6, and 97 for Grades 7 and 8.

In the statement of the rule only 5 per cent of the possible number of errors was made. Only two pupils failed to make some statement. Usually the mistakes consisted of interchanging *q* and *u*.

In spelling the real words no one error seems very important. Failure to follow *q* by *u* occurred 1 per cent of the possible number of times. Fourteen of the seventeen frequencies were in Grades 4 and 5. Omitting *u* in the final syllable *que* occurred 3 per cent of the time. Three of the total of 5 times were in Grades 4 and 5. Since this syllable does not occur in the Gates-Graham list of spelling words before Grade 6, the error is not important.

Adding *u* but dropping the following vowel occurred 0.5 per cent of the time. All except one of these errors were in one section of the fourth grade. Confusing *q* and *g* was found 0.6 per cent of the time. Five of the 9 frequencies were in Grade 4. Since in the study of terms made before any of the rules were taught, the children had been trained in writing the alphabet, it is probable that a class not so drilled would have had more errors in confusing *q* and *g*.

In spelling the nonsense words the same errors occur, only somewhat more frequently. The per cent of the possible number of times that each error occurred is as follows: not following *q* by *u*, 2 per cent; not following *q* by *u* in the final syllable *que*,

TABLE 29

Rule IV—Qu

DISTRIBUTION BY GRADES OF PERCENTAGE OF CHILDREN RECEIVING EACH
SCORE ON THE EXAMINATION AS A WHOLE

SCORE	GRADE				
	4	5	6	7	8
20	30	42	80	79	79
19	33	39	13	12	9
18	14	11	5	9	9
17	12	3	3		3
16	2				
15	2				
14	2				
13					
12	2	3			
11					
10					
9					
8					
7					
6					
5	2				
4					
3					
2		3			
1					
0					
N per Grade	43	36	40	33	33

TABLE 30

Rule IV—Qu

DISTRIBUTION BY GRADES OF PERCENTAGE OF CHILDREN RECEIVING EACH
SCORE ON THE STATEMENT OF THE RULE

SCORE	GRADE				
	4	5	6	7	8
2	84	92	95	100	91
1	5	3			3
0	12	5	5		6
N per Grade	43	36	40	33	33

TABLE 31

Rule IV—Qu

DISTRIBUTION BY GRADES OF PERCENTAGE OF CHILDREN RECEIVING EACH SCORE ON SPELLING REAL WORDS

SCORE	GRADE				
	4	5	6	7	8
8	74	78	97	94	97
7	21	19	3	6	3
6					
5					
4	2				
3					
2					
1	2				
0		3			
N per Grade	43	36	40	33	33

TABLE 32

Rule IV—Qu

DISTRIBUTION BY GRADES OF PERCENTAGE OF CHILDREN RECEIVING EACH SCORE ON SPELLING NONSENSE WORDS

SCORE	GRADE				
	4	5	6	7	8
10	53	61	85	79	88
9	30	33	15	18	9
8	7			3	3
7	5				
6					
5					
4	2				
3					
2	2	3			
1					
0					
N per Grade	43	36	40	33	33

5 per cent; adding *u* but dropping the following vowel, 0.9 per cent; confusing *q* and *g*, 0.6 per cent.

In the nonsense words omitting the *u* occurs throughout the grades but more frequently in the lower grades. Eighteen of the

TABLE 33

Rule IV—Qu

DISTRIBUTION BY MENTAL AGES OF PERCENTAGE OF CHILDREN RECEIVING EACH SCORE ON THE EXAMINATION AS A WHOLE

SCORE	MENTAL AGE						
	9	10	11	12	13	14	15
20	25	40	56	63	62	80	91
19	46	25	33	15	12	11	4
18	13	17	9	10	20	9	
17	8	8	2	8	4		4
16	4			2			
15		3					
14	4	2					
13							
12		2		2			
11							
10					2		
9							
8							
7							
6							
5		2					
4							
3							
2		2					
1							
0							
N per Age	24	60	54	48	50	46	23

TABLE 34

Rule IV—Qu

DISTRIBUTION BY MENTAL AGES OF PERCENTAGE OF CHILDREN RECEIVING EACH SCORE ON THE STATEMENT OF THE RULE

SCORE	MENTAL AGE								
	8	9	10	11	12	13	14	15	16
2	71	86	85	96	96	86	96	100	94
1		8	2	2	2	6	2		
0	28	4	13	2	2	8	2		6
N per Age	7	24	60	54	48	50	46	23	16

TABLE 35

Rule IV—Qu

DISTRIBUTION BY MENTAL AGES OF PERCENTAGE OF CHILDREN RECEIVING
EACH SCORE ON SPELLING REAL WORDS

SCORE	MENTAL AGE								
	8	9	10	11	12	13	14	15	16
8	86	71	78	85	92	92	93	100	100
7	14	25	15	15	6	6	7		
6			2		2	2			
5									
4		4	2						
3									
2									
1			2						
0			2						
N per Age.	7	24	60	54	48	50	46	23	16

TABLE 36

Rule IV—Qu

DISTRIBUTION BY MENTAL AGES OF PERCENTAGE OF CHILDREN RECEIVING
EACH SCORE ON SPELLING NONSENSE WORDS

SCORE	MENTAL AGE								
	8	9	10	11	12	13	14	15	16
10	57	46	57	72	71	78	87	91	87
9	43	33	22	22	15	14	11	4	13
8		17	13	6	8	6	2	4	
7		4	3		4	2			
6									
5									
4			2						
3									
2			2		2				
1									
0			2			2			
N per Age.	7	24	60	54	48	50	46	23	16

23 cases of omitting *u* in the final syllable *que* occur in Grades 4 and 5, where this syllable is not found in the spelling list. Fourteen of the fifteen cases of adding *u* but dropping the following vowel occur in Grades 4 and 5.

The distribution of scores by mental ages showed the same general trend as that by grades. The percentage of children of a given mental age missing one point or less on the examination as a whole was 65 for mental age 10, 89 for 11, 78 for 12, 74 for 13, 91 for 14, and 96 for 15.

Since the errors made on the *qu* rule are so few and unimportant, it seems useless to consider their relation to mental ages.

Probably this rule can be successfully taught in any grade and to any mental age that will be spelling words governed by it.

INTERPRETATION OF DATA FOR RULE V

Rule—I before e
Except after c
Or when sounded as ā
As in neighbor and weigh. (See Tables 37–44.)

In the scores for the total examination (see Table 37) the percentage of children missing one point or less was 17 for Grade 5, 40 for Grade 6, 32 for Grade 7, and 53 for Grade 8. The relatively high score for Grade 6 was due to the fact that one sixth grade had studied this rule in its language book. The difference in achievement between the fifth and the sixth grades was further increased by the fact that the teacher of one section of the fifth grade evidently did not teach all of the rule.

In a tabulation of results the *ie* rule is one of the two rules that showed the statement of the rule superior to the spelling of words. The percentage of children receiving perfect scores on this part of the test was 49 for Grade 5, 83 for Grade 6, 94 for Grade 7, and 82 for Grade 8. Probably the rhyme made the rule easy to remember.

Grades 6, 7, and 8 scored almost equally well and each scored better than Grade 5. The percentage of children misspelling one nonsense word or less was 43 for Grade 5, 63 for Grade 6, 61 for Grade 7, and 65 for Grade 8. The real words scored relatively higher in the upper grades, due probably to general spelling ability.

A study of errors showed that the only significant one in the statement of the rule was in the phrase "Or when sounded as ā as in *neighbor* and *weigh*." This was called wrong if the *ei* part of the words neighbor and weigh was misspelled, since this showed a lack of understanding of the meaning of the rule. Omissions and misspellings of this part of the rule constituted 80 per cent

TABLE 37

Rule V—Ie and ei

DISTRIBUTION BY GRADES OF PERCENTAGE OF CHILDREN RECEIVING EACH
SCORE ON THE EXAMINATION AS A WHOLE

SCORE	GRADE			
	5	6	7	8
21	9	33	23	32
20	9	8	10	21
19	3	18	19	9
18	6	8	6	15
17	23	5	10	6
16	14	23	3	3
15	11	5	13	6
14	11		6	
13	11	3		
12			6	
11	3			
10			3	
9				
8				3
7				3
0				
N per Grade	35	40	31	34

TABLE 38

Rule V—Ie and ei

DISTRIBUTION BY GRADES OF PERCENTAGE OF CHILDREN RECEIVING EACH
SCORE ON THE STATEMENT OF THE RULE

SCORE	GRADE			
	5	6	7	8
4	49	83	94	82
3	42	18	3	6
2	9			
1				
0			3	12
N per Grade	35	40	31	34

TABLE 39

Rule V—Ie and ei

DISTRIBUTION BY GRADES OF PERCENTAGE OF CHILDREN RECEIVING EACH SCORE ON SPELLING REAL WORDS

SCORE	GRADE			
	5	6	7	8
9	17	60	35	65
8	14	10	19	15
7	31	13	3	9
6	37	13	35	6
5		3	3	3
4		3		
3			3	
2				
1				
0				3
N per Grade	35	40	31	34

TABLE 40

Rule V—Ie and ei

DISTRIBUTION BY GRADES OF PERCENTAGE OF CHILDREN RECEIVING EACH SCORE ON SPELLING NONSENSE WORDS

SCORE	GRADE			
	5	6	7	8
8	14	38	29	47
7	29	25	32	18
6	14	23	13	15
5	20	10	16	6
4	17	5	3	
3	3		3	6
2	3		3	3
1				
0				6
N per Grade	35	40	31	34

of all errors and occurred 12 per cent of the possible number. The error was found mostly in Grade 5 where it was the only error, and was made 30 per cent of the time.

An examination of the rule shows that three main types of

TABLE 41

Rule V—Ie and ei

DISTRIBUTION BY MENTAL AGES OF PERCENTAGE OF CHILDREN RECEIVING
EACH SCORE ON THE EXAMINATION AS A WHOLE

SCORE	MENTAL AGE					
	10	11	12	13	14	15
21	11	11	24	27	36	30
20	11	6	12	18	7	22
19	11	6	7	10	11	13
18	6	3	7	4	13	17
17	17	11	14	6	11	
16	6	28	14	10	2	4
15	17	14	2	8	13	
14	11	8	5	8	2	
13	6	8	5	8		
12			2		2	4
11		3	2			
10		3	2			
9	6					
8						4
7			2		7	
6						
5						
4						
3						
2						
1						
0						4
N per Age	18	36	42	49	45	23

errors can be made in the spelling of words, one with *ie*, another
with *ei* after *c*, and a third with *ei* sounded as ā. All of these
errors occurred throughout the grades.

In spelling real words errors in the order of *ie* made up 25 per
cent of all errors and occurred 11 per cent of the possible number
of times. Errors in *ei* sounded as ā made up 38 per cent of all
errors and occurred 19 per cent of the time. Errors in *ei* after *c*
constituted 29 per cent of all errors and occurred 14 per cent of
the time.

In the nonsense words the same kinds of errors occurred but
more frequently. The percentage of possible number of times
that each occurred was 16 for *ie*, 25 for *ei* sounded as ā, and 16
for *ei* after *c*.

TABLE 42

Rule V—Ie and ei

DISTRIBUTION BY MENTAL AGES OF PERCENTAGE OF CHILDREN RECEIVING EACH SCORE ON THE STATEMENT OF THE RULE

SCORE	MENTAL AGE							
	9	10	11	12	13	14	15	16
4	17	56	58	69	77	87	83	83
3	83	28	33	24	20	9	4	17
2		11	8	2	2			
1					2			
0		6		2		4	13	
N per Age	6	18	36	42	49	45	23	12

TABLE 43

Rule V—Ie and ei

DISTRIBUTION BY MENTAL AGES OF PERCENTAGE OF CHILDREN RECEIVING EACH SCORE ON SPELLING REAL WORDS

SCORE	MENTAL AGE							
	9	10	11	12	13	14	15	16
9	33	28	28	43	46	56	52	67
8	33	11	14	9	16	18	26	16
7	17	28	22	17	12	9	4	
6		28	33	21	18	11	9	
5		6		5	2	7	4	8
4					6			
3	17		3	2				
2				2				
1								
0							4	8
N per Age	6	18	36	42	49	45	23	12

The distribution by mental ages for the examination as a whole showed mediocre achievement but gradual increase. The 45 cases of mental age 14 had 43 per cent who missed one point or less. The 23 cases at mental age 15 had 52 per cent who made a similar score.

The distribution of scores by mental ages for the three parts of the examination indicate that the results are similar to those

TABLE 44

Rule V—Ie and ei

DISTRIBUTION BY MENTAL AGES OF PERCENTAGE OF CHILDREN RECEIVING
EACH SCORE ON SPELLING NONSENSE WORDS

SCORE	MENTAL AGE							
	9	10	11	12	13	14	15	16
8		22	11	31	39	47	43	42
7	33	28	22	26	18	11	17	33
6	17	11	17	14	20	22	13	8
5	17	28	19	14	14	7	13	
4		6	19	5	4	4	4	
3	17		8	10	4	2	4	8
2	17	6	3			4		
1								
0						2	4	8
N per Age	6	18	36	42	49	45	23	12

found for the grades. Since so many errors were found throughout the grades and mental ages it hardly seems profitable to try
to locate specific errors by mental ages.

An analysis of the words in the Gates-Graham spelling list
governed by the *ie* rule discloses some interesting facts. If all
ie words that are derivatives formed according to the rule for
changing *y* to *i* were excluded from the list, 76 words would
remain. These would be scattered throughout Grades 2 to 8.
Among these 76 words there would be 13 cases of *ei* sounding as
ā in Grades 2 to 8. There would be also 8 cases of *ei* following
c. This would leave 55 words in which the *i* precedes the *e*.

In view of the small number of words in which *ei* sounds as ā,
it would seem that this part of the rule should be discarded. Like-
wise it would seem more profitable to teach the *cei* words without reference to the rule. If these two parts of the rule were
discarded, all words governed by them would become exceptions
to the *ie* part. This would give 38 exceptions and 55 words following the rule. These considerations raise some doubts whether
any part of the *ie-ei* rule is worth teaching.

INTERPRETATION OF DATA FOR RULE VI

*Rule—The sound of i at the end of a word is usually spelled
by the letter y.* (See Tables 45–52.)

The distribution of scores on the examination as a whole showed that Grades 5 to 7 scored higher than Grades 3 and 4. The percentage of children missing one point or less was 13 for Grade 3, 11 for Grade 4, 31 for Grade 5, 35 for Grade 6, and 34 for Grade 7.

The distribution of scores on the three sections of the rule showed that the grades scored higher on the statement of the rule than in the spelling of words. All the grades spelled the nonsense words almost, if not quite, as well as the real words. Here again Grades 5 to 7 scored noticeably higher than Grades 3 and 4. None of the grades was highly successful in applying the rule. The percentage of children missing one word or less in the nonsense

TABLE 45

Rule VI—Sound of i Spelled y

DISTRIBUTION BY GRADES OF PERCENTAGE OF CHILDREN RECEIVING EACH SCORE ON THE EXAMINATION AS A WHOLE

SCORE	GRADE				
	3	4	5	6	7
24	6	3	8	24	25
23	6	9	22	12	9
22	4	6	28	15	9
21	7	11	3	6	9
20	7	9	14	9	
19	13	9	3	15	13
18	4	14	3	9	6
17	9	9	3	3	9
16	2				6
15	9		3	3	
14	4		8		3
13	2	3	3		3
12	7	9	3		
11		3		3	
10		3			3
9	2	6		3	3
8	4	3			
7	4				
6	2	6			
5	4				
4	2				
0					
N per Grade	46	35	36	34	32

TABLE 46

Rule VI—Sound of i Spelled y

DISTRIBUTION BY GRADES OF PERCENTAGE OF CHILDREN RECEIVING EACH
SCORE ON THE STATEMENT OF THE RULE

SCORE	GRADE				
	3	4	5	6	7
4	35	31	69	76	75
3	20	26	17	18	19
2	15	14	6		3
1	11	3	8		
0	20	26		6	3
N per Grade	46	35	36	34	32

TABLE 47

Rule VI—Sound of i Spelled y

DISTRIBUTION BY GRADES OF PERCENTAGE OF CHILDREN RECEIVING EACH
SCORE ON SPELLING REAL WORDS

SCORE	GRADE				
	3	4	5	6	7
10	15	20	44	44	38
9	22	17	17	18	16
8	15	26	14	6	6
7	20	17	19	24	22
6	9	9		6	6
5	11	9	3		6
4					
3	2			3	3
2	2	3	3		3
1	4				
0					
N per Grade	46	35	36	34	32

words was 31 for Grade 3, 37 for Grade 4, 61 for Grade 5, 56 for
Grade 6, and 40 for Grade 7.

The tabulation of errors showed that each of the four parts of
the rule was missed at least 9 per cent of the time. Most of the
errors occurred in Grades 3, 4, and 5.

In order to try the children's ability to apply the rule, the

TABLE 48

Rule VI—Sound of i Spelled y

DISTRIBUTION BY GRADES OF PERCENTAGE OF CHILDREN RECEIVING EACH
SCORE ON SPELLING NONSENSE WORDS

SCORE	GRADE				
	3	4	5	6	7
10	20	20	25	38	34
9	11	17	36	18	6
8	15	20	17	24	25
7	11	11	11	15	16
6	11	6	6		9
5	7		3		6
4	2	3	3		
3	13	6			
2					3
1		6		6	
0	11	11			
N per Grade	46	35	36	34	32

experimenter put into the test, words that were misspelled in the final *y* part. These words ended in *ey, e,* and *ie.* Among the real words there were three ending in *ey.* These should have been changed to end in *y* only. Many of the children thought that *ey* was correct and did not change it. Since 191 children took the test, there were 573 chances to make this error. It was actually made 30 per cent of this possible number. This error was spread throughout the grades. In proportion to the number of children it occurred as often in Grade 7 as in Grade 3.

Similar words ending in *e,* although they occurred the same number of times, were thought to be right only about one-sixth as often.

In the nonsense words the error of not changing final *ey* to *y* was again most important. Here also it occurred 30 per cent of the possible number of times and again it was found as often in Grade 7 as in Grade 3. The error of not changing final *e* to *y* with the same number of chances was made only one-fifth as many times.

When the distribution of scores by mental ages was consulted, there was found a slight increase of score with increase in age. Mental ages 9 and 10 showed most scattering. This was to be

TABLE 49

Rule VI—Sound of i Spelled y

DISTRIBUTION BY MENTAL AGES OF PERCENTAGE OF CHILDREN RECEIVING
EACH SCORE ON THE EXAMINATION AS A WHOLE

SCORE	MENTAL AGE						
	8	9	10	11	12	13	14
24		12	12	14	21	11	22
23	4	6	15	14	8	11	7
22	13	2	15	22	6	11	11
21		6	15	2	13	8	11
20	13	4	7	12	17	5	11
19	4	12	7	6	15	8	22
18	4	16	5	4	9	21	4
17	9	8	5	2	2	5	4
16		2	2	2	2		
15		8		4		3	
14	9	4	5	6		5	
13	9		2	2	2	5	
12	9	2	5	6			
11			2		2	5	
10		2			2		4
9		6				2	3	4
8	9	2					
7	9	2					
6		2		5			
5		2					
4	4	4					
3							
2							
1	4						
0							
N per Age	23	51	41	49	47	38	27

expected since these were the average mental ages for Grades 3 and 4.

It will be noticed that most of the trouble in spelling these final *y* words was with the ending *ey*. This looks *right* to the children. Probably drill needs to be centered on this error. Since there are several common words that are correctly spelled with final *ey*, care must be taken that the children do not think that *ey* is always wrong.

In view of the fact that the spelling list used in this experiment contains 330 words governed by this rule and scattered throughout Grades 2 to 8, and in view of the additional fact that these

TABLE 50

Rule VI—Sound of i Spelled y

DISTRIBUTION BY MENTAL AGES OF PERCENTAGE OF CHILDREN RECEIVING EACH SCORE ON THE STATEMENT OF THE RULE

SCORE	MENTAL AGE								
	8	9	10	11	12	13	14	15	16
4	30	41	58	63	64	74	81	78	63
3	22	20	17	16	17	21	15	11	13
2	22	10	7	8	11			11	13
1	9	8		4	4				13
0	17	22	17	8	4	5	4		
N per Age .	23	51	41	49	47	38	27	9	8

TABLE 51

Rule VI—Sound of i Spelled y

DISTRIBUTION BY MENTAL AGES OF PERCENTAGE OF CHILDREN RECEIVING EACH SCORE ON SPELLING REAL WORDS

SCORE	MENTAL AGE								
	8	9	10	11	12	13	14	15	16
10	17	16	29	44	47	24	26	56	13
9	13	24	20	14	15	21	26	11	13
8	9	18	24	12	6	18	18	11	13
7	13	24	12	22	19	16	22	22	63
6	13	6	7		6	16			
5	22	2	2	4	6		4		
4		4		4					
3	4		2			3	4		
2		4		2		3			
1	9	4							
0			2						
N per Age .	23	51	41	49	47	38	27	9	8

words are so frequently misspelled in nearly all grades, it would seem advisable to use this rule if it can be made to function reasonably well.

There are probably at least two reasons that may account for the difficulty of the rule. One is that children may tend to spell visually instead of phonetically. Another is that words ending

TABLE 52

Rule VI—Sound of i Spelled y

DISTRIBUTION BY MENTAL AGES OF PERCENTAGE OF CHILDREN RECEIVING
EACH SCORE ON SPELLING NONSENSE WORDS

SCORE	MENTAL AGE								
	8	9	10	11	12	13	14	15	16
10	9	22	27	27	36	21	33	22	
9	13	14	27	22	17	13	7	33	
8	13	14	15	27	23	13	41	33	50
7	9	12	12	10	17	26	7	11	25
6	9	12	2	6	2	11	7		13
5	9	6		4		5			
4	4	4	5	2		3			13
3	22	8		2					
2					2		4		
1		2	2		2	5			
0	13	8	12			3			
N per Age .	22	51	41	49	47	38	27	9	8

in the short sound of *i* are commonly mispronounced both by children and by teachers.

In this experiment the final sound of the *i* rule was taught in three lessons including the examination. No doubt more time should have been spent on drill in applying the rule. The large number of words concerned would easily justify more time. It may be that no attempt should be made to teach the rule before Grade 5.

INTERPRETATION OF DATA FOR RULE VII

Rule—Words of one syllable and words with the accent on the last syllable ending in one consonant preceded by one vowel, double the final consonant when adding a suffix beginning with a vowel. (See Tables 53–61.)

None of the grades did well on this rule, although Grades 6 to 8 scored much higher than Grade 5. In this test which had a highest score of only 26, Grade 5 had only one child who scored as high as 23. All the others missed at least 7 points. Almost half the children scored 13 or below.

Grades 6, 7, and 8 showed only slight, if any, improvement from grade to grade. The range of scores and the mid-score were very

TABLE 53

Rule VII—Doubling Final Consonant

DISTRIBUTION BY GRADES OF PERCENTAGE OF CHILDREN RECEIVING EACH
SCORE ON THE EXAMINATION AS A WHOLE

SCORE	GRADE			
	5	6	7	8
26		7	3	10
25		7	9	7
24		5	6	20
23	3	5	11	3
22		12	14	7
21		5	11	13
20		10	9	3
19	3	10	6	
18	3	7	9	7
17	9	5		7
16	9	7	3	7
15	9	5	11	3
14	18	12		3
13	18	2	3	10
12	24		6	
11		2		
10	6			
0				
N per Grade	34	42	35	30

nearly the same. These highest three grades each had a range of
about 14 points. Very few pupils received high scores. The percentage of each grade that missed one point or less on the examination as a whole was 14 for Grade 6, 11 for Grade 7, and 17 for
Grade 8.

The tabulation by grades of the scores on the statement of the
rule showed great differences in the amounts learned by different
sections of the same grades. One sixth-grade section had only
one score that was not above the highest score obtained by another
section. One of the eighth grades had only one score above the
lowest score obtained by one seventh grade. When all sections of
one grade are grouped together, the sixth, seventh, and eighth
grades have 36, 37, and 37 per cent of correct answers on the
statement of the rule.

An examination of errors made in the statement of the rule

TABLE 54

Rule VII—Doubling Final Consonant

DISTRIBUTION BY GRADES OF PERCENTAGE OF CHILDREN RECEIVING EACH
SCORE ON THE STATEMENT OF THE RULE

SCORE	GRADE			
	5	6	7	8
6		36	37	37
5		7	26	7
4	6	14	20	20
3	6	7	11	13
2	26	26	6	7
1	41	5		
0	21	5		17
N per Grade	34	42	35	30

TABLE 55

Rule VII—Doubling Final Consonant

DISTRIBUTION BY GRADES OF PERCENTAGE OF CHILDREN RECEIVING EACH
SCORE ON SPELLING REAL WORDS

SCORE	GRADE			
	5	6	7	8
10	6	28	31	53
9	12	31	31	23
8	23	26	11	10
7	21	12	11	10
6	29	2	8	3
5	6		6	
4	3			
3				
2				
1				
0				
N per Grade	34	42	35	30

showed that the low-scoring eighth grade seemed to have learned
the rule as "Words of one syllable and words with the accent on
the last syllable double the final consonant." It is difficult to account for these great differences in achievement except on the
basis of differences in teaching.

TABLE 56

Rule VII—Doubling Final Consonant

DISTRIBUTION BY GRADES OF PERCENTAGE OF CHILDREN RECEIVING EACH
SCORE ON SPELLING NONSENSE WORDS

SCORE	GRADE			
	5	6	7	8
10	3	17	8	17
9	3	12	14	23
8		12	11	20
7	18	19	26	10
6	29	17	23	13
5	26	12	6	
4	18	7	3	7
3	3	2	6	10
2			3	
1				
0				
N per Grade	34	42	35	30

TABLE 57

INEFFICIENCY OF SPELLING NONSENSE WORDS GOVERNED BY RULE VII AS
MEASURED BY THE PER CENT OF POSSIBLE NUMBER OF ERRORS MADE

ITEM	GRADE			
	5	6	7	8
1. Doubling final consonant when suffix does not begin with a vowel	59	67	45	34
2. Not doubling final consonant when the accent is on the last syllable	21	17	15	15
3. Doubling final consonant when the word does not end in one consonant	51	24	36	22
4. Doubling final consonant when the consonant is preceded by more than one vowel	39	43	43	41
5. Not doubling final consonant in a monosyllable	36	18	25	16
6. Doubling final consonant when accent is not on last syllable	34	35	39	31

The statement of Rule VII was divided into six parts for scoring. These parts were learned with an inefficiency varying from 9 to 52 per cent for the grades as a whole.

TABLE 58

Rule VII—Doubling Final Consonant

DISTRIBUTION BY MENTAL AGES OF PERCENTAGE OF CHILDREN RECEIVING EACH SCORE ON THE EXAMINATION AS A WHOLE

SCORE	MENTAL AGE						
	10	11	12	13	14	15	16
26			4	6	5	13	20
25	6		4	4	12	17	20
24	6	3	2	4	7	13	
23	6	6	2	2	5	13	20
22		8	7	4	19	4	
21			4	10	7	13	7
20	6	3	7	6	12		
19	6	3	18	8	2		7
18	12	6	7	12	2	9	
17	6	3	9	4	5		7
16		11	9	10	9		7
15	12	8	9	6	2	4	7
14	12	17	9	10	5	4	7
13	12	14	2	8	7	4	
12	6	14	2	4	2	4	
11			2				
10	6	6					
9							
8			2	4			
7							
6							
5							
4	6						
3							
2							
1							
0							
N per Age	17	36	45	51	43	23	15

The percentage of all the grades missing a given part of the rule was as follows:

Part of Rule Missed   *Per Cent*

1. Words of one syllable 9
2. and words with the accent on the last syllable 32
3. ending in one consonant 49
4. preceded by one vowel 52
5. double the final consonant 15
6. when adding a suffix beginning with a vowel 34

TABLE 59

Rule VII—Doubling Final Consonant

DISTRIBUTION BY MENTAL AGES OF PERCENTAGE OF CHILDREN RECEIVING
EACH SCORE ON THE STATEMENT OF THE RULE

SCORE	MENTAL AGE							
	9	10	11	12	13	14	15	16
6	17	12	11	31	20	28	43	47
5		6	8	9	10	19	13	13
4	17	12	8	7	14	14	17	20
3	33	18		9	10	12	13	13
2	17	18	25	24	35	19	9	
1	17	18	33	7	2			
0		18	14	13	10	9	4	7
N per Age	6	17	36	45	51	43	23	15

TABLE 60

Rule VII—Doubling Final Consonant

DISTRIBUTION BY MENTAL AGES OF PERCENTAGE OF CHILDREN RECEIVING
EACH SCORE ON SPELLING REAL WORDS

SCORE	MENTAL AGE							
	9	10	11	12	13	14	15	16
10		24	19	22	22	35	65	53
9	33	6	17	20	20	30	17	27
8	33	18	19	38	20	12	4	20
7	33	29	17	13	22	14	4	
6	17	12	19	4	12	7	4	
5	17	6	6		6	2	4	
4			3	2				
3								
2		6						
1								
0								
N per Age	6	17	36	45	51	43	23	15

Of course the grades differed in efficiency of learning. In general some improvement was made from grade to grade, but every part of the rule was missed at least once by every grade.

The success of the application of the rule as measured by the spelling of nonsense words is shown in Table 57. Since the per-

TABLE 61

Rule VII—Doubling Final Consonant

DISTRIBUTION BY MENTAL AGES OF PERCENTAGE OF CHILDREN RECEIVING
EACH SCORE ON SPELLING NONSENSE WORDS

SCORE	MENTAL AGE							
	9	10	11	12	13	14	15	16
10		12		7	10	19	17	27
9		6	6	9	14	19	30	20
8	33	6	6	4	12	12	17	13
7		18	19	29	18	23	13	7
6	33	12	22	29	27	14	9	13
5	17	24	25	9	6	9		
4	17	18	19	4	6		4	20
3			3	4	4	2	9	
2		6		2		2		
1								
0				2	4			
N per Age	6	17	36	45	51	43	23	15

centages are measures of error, the smaller numbers show greater success. Items 4 and 6 show little, if any, improvement from grade to grade. The smallest percentage of error is 15 made on item 2 in Grades 7 and 8. The highest is 67 made on item 1 in Grade 6.

Five periods of approximately fifteen minutes each were spent in teaching this rule. There are 45 words governed by it in Grades 2 to 8. Fourteen of these are in Grades 2, 3, and 4. This leaves 30 for Grades 5 to 8. At the conservative estimate of 4 words for each fifteen-minute spelling period, 20 words or 67 per cent of these could have been taught in the time used to teach this rule. If the rule is not taught as early as Grade 5 the per cent becomes higher. If left until Grade 7 only 11 words remain.

In consideration of the frequency of words and their grade distribution, the length of time required to teach the rule, and the very unsatisfactory results, it does not seem worth while to teach this particular rule.

CHAPTER VI

SUMMARY AND CONCLUSIONS

In the course of this study seven rules for spelling found in modern spelling books were taught to children in Grades 3 to 8 inclusive. After each teaching period an examination was given in each rule to test the children's ability to remember the rule and to apply it both to real words and to nonsense words. The papers were then analyzed, and the errors studied thoroughly to secure useful suggestions for teaching these rules.

The conclusions reached as a result of this study are treated in this chapter.

GENERAL FINDINGS

1. Efficiency in learning to state and to apply the rules was increased from grade to grade.

2. Scores by mental ages were very similar to those of the grade having the same average mental age.

3. Scores on nonsense words showed the same general errors as the real words, but the mistakes usually were more numerous, probably because the unfamiliarity of the material made reasoning more difficult and because there was no help from words already learned.

FINDINGS FOR RULE I

Rule—Most nouns form their plurals by adding s or es to the singular. Es is added to make the word easier to pronounce.

1. For Rule I, the greatest difficulty was found with adding *es*, both in stating the rule and in spelling the words. Thirty-eight per cent of all children who wrote the rule at all omitted this part.

2. Not only was there a high percentage of possible errors made in adding *es* to form plurals, but also these mistakes were the only ones that occurred at all frequently. The percentage of the possible number of *es* errors made in spelling nonsense words was 76 for Grade 3, 61 for Grade 4, 49 for Grade 5, 27 for Grade 6,

34 for Grade 7, and 36 for Grade 8. The percentage of *es* errors of the total number of errors was found to be 85 for Grade 3, 87 for Grade 4, 95 for Grade 5, 84 for Grade 6, 87 for Grade 7, and 95 for Grade 8.

3. If the statement concerning the adding of *es* is to be included in the rule, to avoid interference it might be better to teach it at a different time from that of adding *s*.

4. Since the list of words commonly taught contains only eight *es* plurals, it may be more economical to teach these words without reference to any rule.

5. If the rule for forming plurals were limited to adding *s*, it could probably be taught in Grade 4 and possibly in Grade 3.

FINDINGS FOR RULE II

Rule—Drop the final e before adding a suffix beginning with a vowel.

1. The errors for this rule were largely those of omissions.

2. Eleven per cent of all children failed to write any part of the rule. This failure constituted about one-third of all errors made in stating the rule.

3. Omitting the phrase "beginning with a vowel" made up 40 per cent of all errors in stating the rule. Fourteen per cent of all children made this mistake. Twenty-two per cent of the children in Grades 3 and 4 omitted this phrase.

4. In spelling real words 31 per cent of all errors were due to omissions of either the suffix or the entire word.

5. In spelling nonsense words 37 per cent of all errors were omissions.

6. Failure to drop final *e* when adding a suffix beginning with a vowel was limited almost entirely to adding the suffix *ing*. Failure to drop *e* was very rare with the suffixes *er* and *ed*. This fact may have been due more to the appearance of the word than to the application of the rule. Probably the two *e*'s that result from not dropping final *e* do not look *right* to the children.

7. In spelling real words 97 per cent of the errors made in failing to drop final *e* when adding *ing* were made in Grades 3 and 4. In the nonsense words this per cent was 88.

8. It was concluded that Rule II could be successfully taught in Grades 3 to 8, if emphasis were placed on adding *ing* in Grades 3 and 4.

FINDINGS FOR RULE III

Rule—When final y is preceded by a consonant, change the y to i before adding any suffix that does not begin with i.

1. In stating the rule the part missed most often was the phrase "before adding any suffix that does not begin with *i*." This error accounted for 45 per cent of all those made in writing the rule.

2. In spelling the words a few children dropped final *y* instead of changing it to *i*. This may have been caused by interference from Rule II which preceded Rule III.

3. The most serious error for Rule III was changing final *y* to *i* when it was not preceded by a consonant. This occurred 30 per cent of the time for real words and 12 per cent for nonsense words. This decrease in errors for nonsense words was unusual.

4. In spelling real words final *y* not preceded by a consonant was changed to *i* 40 per cent of the time in Grade 5, 29 per cent in Grades 6 and 7, and 17 per cent in Grade 8. In the nonsense words all except one of these errors occurred in Grades 5 and 6.

5. It was concluded that this rule could be successfully taught in Grades 5 to 8, if special emphasis were placed on words in which the final *y* is not preceded by a consonant and, therefore, does not change to *i*.

FINDINGS FOR RULE IV

Rule—Q is always followed by u.

1. The scores were generally high for all grades and there was very little scattering of scores.

2. In stating Rule IV, only 5 per cent of the possible number of errors was made. Only two pupils failed to make some statement of the rule.

3. In spelling the words no error was made often enough to be important.

4. It was concluded that Rule IV could be successfully taught in Grades 4 to 8 where the words governed by it occur.

FINDINGS FOR RULE V

Rule—I before e
Except after c
Or when sounded as ā
As in neighbor and weigh.

1. This is one of the two rules for which the statement of the rule scored higher than the spelling of the word. Probably the rhyme made it easy to remember.

2. The principal trouble in stating the rule was with the phrase "Or when sounded as ā as in *neighbor* and *weigh*." The omissions and misspellings of this phrase constituted 80 per cent of all errors made in stating the rule and occurred 12 per cent of the time. It was found mostly in Grade 5 where it was the only error and where it occurred 30 per cent of the time.

3. In the nonsense words errors with *ie* occurred 16 per cent of the time, with *ei* sounded as ā, 25 per cent, and with *cei*, 16 per cent.

4. The Gates-Graham list contains only 13 words having *ei* sounded as ā and only 8 having *cei*. This number hardly justifies teaching a rule that is so hard to apply. If the parts of the rule governing these words were to be dropped, there would be almost as many exceptions as words following.

FINDINGS FOR RULE VI

Rule—The sound of i at the end of a word is usually spelled by the letter y.

1. This is one of the two rules that scored higher in a statement of the rule than in the spelling of the word.

2. Each part in the statement of the rule was missed at least 9 per cent of the time.

3. In both the real and the nonsense words the greatest difficulty was with using final *ey* instead of final *y*. It looked right to the children. This error occurred 30 per cent of the time in both the real and the nonsense words. In proportion to the number of children it occurred as often in Grade 7 as in Grade 3.

4. In view of the large number of words governed by Rule VI and their spread throughout the grades, it seems advisable to give more drill on the application of this rule to determine whether it can be more successfully applied by grade children.

5. In drilling to correct the *ey* error, it will be necessary to take care that serious interference is not set up with words that are exceptions to this rule, and that end in *ey*.

FINDINGS FOR RULE VII

Rule—Words of one syllable and words with the accent on the last syllable ending in one consonant preceded by one vowel, double the final consonant when adding a suffix beginning with a vowel.

1. That this rule is difficult enough to test teaching ability and study habits is evidenced by the great difference in achievement of the different sections of the same grade.

2. The percentage of error in stating the different parts of the rule varied from 9 to 52 per cent for the grades as a whole. Every part of the rule was missed at least once by every grade.

3. In the nonsense words six kinds of errors were made. The average percentage of error for Grades 5 to 7 on each of these kinds ranged from 17 to 51 per cent.

4. The average percentage for the six types of errors by grades was 40 for Grade 5, 34 for Grades 6 and 7, and 27 for Grade 8.

5. Considering the time required to teach the rule and the unsatisfactory results, the conclusion was made that Rule VII as taught in the experiment was not worth while.

It is the judgment of the author that all except two of the rules here tested were understood and applied by grade children with enough success to warrant further study. It seems reasonable to state that Rules V and VII, at least under the conditions of this experiment, did not give evidence of being profitable.

This study does not settle the question of whether these rules should be taught. It aims only to give evidence as to whether children can understand and apply these rules under certain very limited conditions. Further studies should be made to show whether this ability can be made to transfer to everyday spelling. Additional studies are needed to determine whether the words governed by these rules can be taught more successfully by other methods.

APPENDIX I

TEST ON PRELIMINARY TERMS

Name ....Date........................

Teacher's Name ....School ....

  I. Draw a line under the nouns in the following list:

      dog   night   pretty   ran   sunshine   before   trouble

  II. Write the number 1 (one) before each word that is singular.
Write the number 2 (two) before each word that is plural.

babies	head	boxes
bath	drums	danger
children	girls	farmer

  III. Draw a line around each of these letters that is a vowel.

      d   e   a   f   p   i   l   o   t   u

  IV. Draw a line around the consonants.

      h   o   r   c   u   g   k

  V. Draw a line under the double letters in these words:

      dull   funny   see   pen

  VI. Write a number before each of these words to show how many syllables it has.

| happy | sun | grandfather |
| snowflake | crow | buttercup |

  VII. Draw a line under the syllable that is accented in each of these words.

| gingerbread | together |
| birthday | garage |

  VIII. Underline the suffixes in these words:

      miller   mousie   willing

  IX. Draw a line around the final letter of these words:

      nest   green   hollow

  X. What letter precedes "i" in the word "fruit"?

  XI. Write a word that has short "e" and one that has short "i":

    Short "e"................... short "i"...................

  XII. Write the letters of the alphabet.

APPENDIX II

SAMPLE LESSON PLANS FOR RULES VII AND IV

ILLUSTRATION OF A RULE THAT ADDED A SUFFIX

DOUBLING THE FINAL CONSONANT

Rule VII—Words of one syllable and words with the accent on the last syllable ending in one consonant preceded by one vowel, double the final consonant when adding a suffix beginning with a vowel.

LESSON I: DEVELOPMENT OF RULE FOR MONOSYLLABLES

I. Before class time write on the blackboard the following:

Root Word	Suffix	Derivative
. . . .	. . . .	. . . .
. . . .	. . . .	. . . .
. . . .	. . . .	. . . .

(These words will be monosyllables supplied by the office. They will be monosyllables to which Rule VII applies.)

II. When the class is ready to begin, proceed as follows:
  A. Developing the elements of the rule.
    1. Addition of a suffix beginning with a vowel.
      a. Have one child pronounce all the derivatives.
      b. Teacher (pointing to the first root word): "What suffix was added to run to make running?"* (ing.) *One* child responds at a time. If any child says that *ning* was added to running, tell him that the suffix is just *ing.*
      c. Have the class give the suffix added to each word. *One* child responds at a time. *One* child should give *one* suffix. As soon as a suffix is given, the teacher writes it on the blackboard.
      d. Teacher: "Letters are called vowels and consonants. With which of these does each of the suffixes begin?" (Vowels.)
    2. Doubling the final letter.
      a. Teacher: "When run is changed to running, *ing* is added. What else is added to run?"
      b. Class tells what beside the suffix is added to each of the root words to make the derivatives. *One* child takes *one* word.
      c. Teacher: "What was done to all the root words when the suffix beginning with a vowel was added?" (The final letter was doubled.)

* The correct answers to the teacher's questions are suggested in parentheses, after the questions.

66

As soon as the correct answer is given the teacher says, "Yes, the final letter was doubled when the consonant beginning with a vowel was added."

3. Words of one syllable ending in one consonant preceded by one vowel.

   a. Teacher: "You will remember that the parts of a word are called syllables. How many syllables has each of these root words?" (One.)

   b. Teacher: "Letters are called vowels and consonants. With which of these do all the root words end?" (Consonants.)

   c. Teacher: "Yes, all of these root words end in one consonant."

   d. Teacher: "What kind of letter precedes the single consonant?" (Vowel.) Teacher: "Yes, the single consonant is preceded by one vowel."

B. Stating the rule.

  1. Teacher: "We have a spelling rule which says 'Words of one syllable ending in one consonant preceded by one vowel, double the final consonant before a suffix beginning with a vowel'."

  2. If there is extra time the teacher may write the rule on the blackboard and have some of the children try to say it without looking at the blackboard.

Number of minutes spent in teaching lesson. . . . .

Names of absentees. . . . .

For Grades 5 and 6

Words on blackboard for developing rule

Root Word	Suffix	Derivative
1. whip	. . . .	whipping
2. big	. . . .	bigger
3. fun	. . . .	funny
4. rot	. . . .	rotten
5. stop	. . . .	stopped
6. big	. . . .	biggest
7. pup	. . . .	puppy
8. run	. . . .	running

For Grades 7 and 8

Words on blackboard for developing rule

Root Word	Suffix	Derivative
1. win	. . . .	winning
2. wrap	. . . .	wrapped
3. up	. . . .	upper
4. sun	. . . .	sunny
5. stop	. . . .	stopping
6. big	. . . .	bigger
7. put	. . . .	putting
8. big	. . . .	biggest

I. Before class time write on the blackboard the following:

Root Word	Suffix	Derivative
. . . .	. . . .	. . . .
. . . .	. . . .	. . . .
. . . .	. . . .	. . . .

(These words will be supplied by the office. The list will contain monosyllables and words accented on the last syllable, to which Rule VII applies.)

II. When the class is ready to begin, proceed as follows:
A. Developing the new element of the rule—words accented on the last syllable.
1. One child pronounces all the root words.
2. Teacher: "The words in to-day's lesson have more than one syllable. Whenever the words have more than one syllable, there is an accented syllable. On which syllable is the accent in the first word, *compel?*"
3. The class gives the accent for *one* word at a time. The teacher marks the accent on the word.
4. Teacher: "On which syllable is the accent in all these words?" (Last syllable.) "Yes, these words are accented on the last syllable."
B. Reviewing the old elements.
1. Teacher: "Look at the root words and derivatives in these words. How are they like the words we learned yesterday?" (1. End in a single consonant. 2. Preceded by a single vowel. 3. Double the final letter. 4. Before a suffix beginning with a vowel.)
C. Statement of the rule.
1. Teacher: "When we add what we learned to-day to what we learned yesterday, our spelling rule says 'Words of one syllable and words with the accent on the last syllable ending in one consonant preceded by one vowel, double the final consonant when adding a suffix beginning with a vowel.'"
2. Teacher: "I shall write the rule for you." (Teacher writes the rule on the blackboard where all can see.)
D. Drill on the rule.
1. Teacher: "I want to see whether you can remember the rule. I shall ask you for it *again* to-morrow. This rule has six parts. Will you listen while I say it?" Teacher repeats the rule counting off the parts on her fingers as follows: Words of one syllable   and words accented on the last syllable   ending in one consonant   preceded by one vowel,   double the final consonant   when adding a suffix beginning with a vowel. (The spaces indicate pauses.)
2. Five children say the rule, if possible, without looking at the blackboard. Teacher reminds them of the six parts.

Number of minutes spent in teaching lesson. . . . .
Names of absentees. . . . .

For Grades 5 and 6

To be written on the blackboard as an aid in developing the rule—not to be copied by the class

Root Word	Suffix	Derivative
1. beg	....	begged
2. stop	....	stopped
3. cut	....	cutting
4. up	....	upper
5. equip'	....	equipped
6. forgot'	....	forgotten
7. omit'	....	omitted
8. prefer'	....	preferring

For Grades 7 and 8

To be written on the blackboard as an aid in developing the rule—not to be copied by the class

Root Word	Suffix	Derivative
1. fit	....	fitted
2. rot	....	rotten
3. pup	....	puppy
4. shop	....	shopping
5. forgot'	....	forgotten
6. omit'	....	omitting
7. begin'	....	beginning
8. compel'	....	compelled

LESSON III: ORAL APPLICATION OF THE RULE

I. Before class time write on the blackboard the following:
   A. Statement of rule.
   B. Root words to be changed to derivatives.

Root Word	Suffix	Derivative
....	....	....
....	....	....
....	....	....

(These words will be supplied by the office. The list will contain monosyllables and words accented on the last syllable, some of which double the final consonant, and some of which do not.)

II. When the class is ready to begin, proceed as follows:
   A. Drill on the rule.
      1. Have five pupils repeat the rule, if possible, without looking at the blackboard.
   B. Application of rule.
      1. Turn to list of words on the blackboard. Have one child read all the root words.
      2. Have class spell the derivatives formed by adding the suffixes to the root words. *One* child should spell *one* derivative. Teacher writes the derivatives on the blackboard.

Before beginning to spell the derivatives the teacher says, "We shall have many things to think of to-day. Let us look at the blackboard to be sure of what the rule says. (Turns to rule and numbers the parts as she calls attention to them.) "First we must look to see whether we have a word of one syllable (No. 1). If it isn't a word of one syllable, we must see whether it is a word accented on the last syllable (No. 2). Then does it end in *one* consonant (No. 3) and is it preceded by *one* vowel (No. 4)? Then we must see whether the suffix begins with a vowel (No. 5). If it does all of these things, we double the final consonant (No. 6). There are many things to remember."

3. After a child spells a derivative ask him why he spelled it that way. If the word is misspelled, point out the part of the rule which was violated and have the child spell the derivative correctly.

Number of minutes spent in teaching lesson. . . . .

Names of absentees. . . . .

For Grades 5 and 6

Words for class drill—not to be copied by the children

Root Word	Suffix	Derivative
1. can	ed	. . . .
2. clip	ing	. . . .
3. seal	ed	. . . .
4. sun	less	. . . .
5. gum	y	. . . .
6. appeal'	ing	. . . .
7. submit'	ed	. . . .
8. an'chor	ing	. . . .
9. suggest'	ion	. . . .
10. excel'	ent	. . . .
11. refer'	ed	. . . .
12. bal'lot	ing	. . . .
13. enjoy'	ment	. . . .
14. attest'	ed	. . . .

For Grades 7 and 8

Words for class drill—not to be copied by the children

Root Word	Suffix	Derivative
1. plan	ed	. . . .
2. war	ior	. . . .
3. sun	less	. . . .
4. can	ed	. . . .
5. submit'	ing	. . . .
6. remit'	ance	. . . .
7. cov'er	ed	. . . .
8. appoint'	ed	. . . .
9. refer'	ed	. . . .
10. attest'	ing	. . . .

11. appear'	ance	....
12. jour'nal	ism	....
13. await'	ing	....
14. enjoy'	ment	....

LESSON IV: WRITTEN APPLICATION OF THE RULE

I. Before class time write the rule on the blackboard. Number the parts as they were numbered yesterday.

II. When the class is ready to begin, proceed as follows:

A. Drill on rule.

1. Have five pupils repeat the rule, if possible, without looking at the blackboard. Call attention to the six parts of the rule.

B. Written application of rule.

1. Pass out mimeographed sheets.

When passing out the mimeographed sheets the teacher says that the rule may be written on the back of the sheet after the derivatives are written. The children may look at the blackboard if they find it necessary.

2. The children will probably make so many mistakes that it will not be profitable to try to help them while they are writing. Instead, as soon as all the children have begun to write the rule have the class stop writing. The teacher should then spell the derivatives. Each child should correct his own paper. After each word is spelled the children who have made mistakes should raise their hands. The child who has made a mistake should be asked why he spelled the word that way. The part of the rule violated should then be pointed out and the child should spell the derivative correctly.

3. If time permits, have the children finish writing the rule.

Number of minutes spent in teaching lesson..............................

Names of absentees..

For Grades 5 and 6

Root Word	Suffix	Derivative
1. rob	ery	....
2. tat	ing	....
3. bag	age	....
4. mad	ly	....
5. brief	est	....
6. remit'	ance	....
7. behold'	ing	....
8. transfer'	ed	....
9. gar'den	ing	....
10. disgust'	ed	....
11. regret'	ed	....
12. succeed'	ed	....
13. jour'nal	ism	....
14. allot'	ment	....

For Grades 7 and 8

Root Word	Suffix	Derivative
1. bag	age	....
2. ship	ed	....
3. job	er	....
4. mad	ly	....
5. transfer'	ed	....
6. regret'	ed	....
7. succeed'	ed	....
8. disgust'	ed	....
9. an'chor	ed	....
10. bal'lot	ing	....
11. compel'	ed	....
12. appeal'	ing	....
13. allot'	ment	....
14. suggest'	ion	....

TEST ON DOUBLING FINAL CONSONANTS

Name..Date..................

I. On the back of this sheet write the spelling rule about doubling the final consonant. If you cannot spell a word write it the best that you can.

II. Fill in the derivatives by adding the suffixes to the root words.

Root Word	Suffix	Derivative
1. trim	ed	....
2. wed	ing	....
3. slip	ery	....
4. glad	ness	....
5. refer'	ing	....
6. rebel'	ion	....
7. commit'	ed	....
8. appear'	ance	....
9. amount'	ed	....
10. ham'mer	ing	....

III. These are not real words. Make believe that they are. Make words by adding the suffixes to the root words. Write the new words under Derivative.

Root Word	Suffix	Derivative
1. bam	ing	....
2. dus	ed	....
3. fren	ance	....
4. duf	ly	....
5. reprob'	ing	....
6. fosot'	ed	....
7. lifost'	er	....
8. gar'fet	ed	....
9. kaef	ing	....
10. behuf'	er	....

ILLUSTRATION OF RULE GOVERNING THE BODY OF WORDS

QU RULE

Rule IV—Q is always followed by u.

LESSON I

I. Before class time write on the blackboard the following list of words:

A. ....

....

....

(The words to be used here will be given to each section of each grade.)

B. *Qu* words misspelled.

....

....

....

(These words will be supplied for the classes.)

II. When the class is ready to begin, proceed as follows:

A. Developing the elements of the rule.

  1. Have one child pronounce all the words.

  2. Teacher: "What is the same about all of these words?" (The answers should include the fact that each word has a *q* and a *u* and that *q* is followed by *u*. If these points are not given in answer to the first question additional questions will be necessary.)

B. Stating the rule.

  1. Teacher: "There is a spelling rule that says, *q* is always followed by *u*. I shall write it on the blackboard." (She writes rule where all can see.)

C. Drill on rule.

  1. Teacher has five children repeat the rule, if possible, without looking at the blackboard.

D. Application of rule.

  1. Teacher (turning to the *qu* words misspelled): "Here are some words that are not spelled correctly according to the *qu* rule. Tell me how to spell them correctly." (One child spells one word. Teacher writes correct form on blackboard.)

  2. Teacher (passing out mimeographed sheets): "Here are some more words that are misspelled according to the *qu* rule. Rewrite them correctly. If you have more time, try to write the rule without looking at the blackboard." Teacher should move about the room to see that everyone has understood.

Number of minutes spent in teaching lesson.............................

Names of absentees..

For Grades 5 and 6

	Wrong	*Right*
1.	qotation	....
2.	eqally	....
3.	liqid	....

4. qantity   ....
5. qarter   ....
6. liqor   ....
7. sqeeze   ....
8. bouqet   ....
9. picturesqe   ....
10. chautauqa   ....

For Grades 7 and 8

	Wrong	*Right*
1.	freqency	....
2.	antiqity	....
3.	eqity	....
4.	eqality	....
5.	burlesqe	....
6.	conseqent	....
7.	etiqette	....
8.	picturesqe	....
9.	sqeeze	....
10.	chautauqa	....

TEST ON QU RULE

Name...Date...............

I. Write the *qu* rule for spelling. If you cannot spell a word write it the best that you can.

II. These words are not spelled right. Write them as they should be.

	Wrong	*Right*
1.	reqest	....
2.	conqest	....
3.	freqent	....
4.	qarrel	....
5.	conqer	....
6.	banqet	....
7.	antiqe	....
8.	quality	....

III. These are not real words. Make believe that they are. Some of them are wrong. Spell them as the *qu* rule says they should be spelled.

	Wrong	*Right*
1.	qan	....
2.	sqid	....
3.	quat	....
4.	graqe	....
5.	seqarit	....
6.	fraqis	....
7.	quiges	....
8.	qartegar	....
9.	biqante	....
10.	topasqe	....

NOTE: The children knew that some correct words were included in the list.

APPENDIX III

FINAL EXAMINATIONS ON RULES I, II, III, V, AND VI

RULE I—PLURALS

Name...Date...............

I. Write the rule that tells how to form the plural of nouns from the singular. If you cannot spell a word, write it the best that you can.

II. Change each of these singular nouns to plural nouns.

1. slipper   ....
2. class   ....
3. case   ....
4. note   ....
5. charge   ....
6. peach   ....
7. price   ....
8. meeting   ....
9. wish   ....

III. These are not real words. Make believe they are singular nouns. Say them to yourself so the other boys and girls cannot hear them. Then add *s* or *es* to each one to make a plural.

1. fatch   ....
2. dat   ....
3. sep   ....
4. runce   ....
5. luss   ....
6. bea   ....
7. fuce   ....
8. bish   ....
9. farge   ....

RULE II—DROPPING FINAL *e*

Name...Date...............

I. Write the spelling rule that we learned yesterday. If you cannot spell a word write it the best that you can.

II. Fill in the derivatives by adding the suffix to the root word.

Root Word	Suffix	Derivative
1. lace	ed	....
2. close	ing	....
3. hate	ed	....
4. please	ing	

	Root Word	Suffix	Derivative
5.	invite	ed	. . . .
6.	inclose	ed	. . . .
7.	welcome	ing	. . . .
8.	bake	ing	. . . .
9.	strange	er	. . . .
10.	lose	er	. . . .

III. These are not real words. Make believe that they are. Make new words by adding the suffixes to the root words. Write the new words under Derivative.

	Root Word	Suffix	Derivative
1.	hace	ing	. . . .
2.	fide	ed	. . . .
3.	brafe	er	. . . .
4.	garbe	ing	. . . .
5.	joble	ing	. . . .
6.	maske	ing	. . . .
7.	flale	ed	. . . .
8.	rutipe	ed	. . . .
9.	znobe	ing	. . . .
10.	bofoupe	er	. . . .

RULE III—CHANGING *y* TO *i*

Name. . . . . .Date. . . . .

I. Write the spelling rule about changing *y* to *i*. If you cannot spell a word, write it the best that you can.

II. Fill in the derivative by adding the suffix to the root word.

	Root Word	Suffix	Derivative
1.	ferry	es	. . . .
2.	bury	ed	. . . .
3.	beauty	ful	. . . .
4.	curly	er	. . . .
5.	silly	est	. . . .
6.	hurry	ing	. . . .
7.	envy	ous	. . . .
8.	steady	ly	. . . .
9.	deny	able	. . . .
10.	holy	ness	. . . .
11.	display	ed	. . . .

III. These are not real words. Make believe that they are. Make new words by adding the suffixes to the root words. Write the new words under Derivative.

	Root Word	Suffix	Derivative
1.	hry	ed	. . . .
2.	psy	est	. . . .
3.	fardy	er	. . . .
4.	vaply	es	. . . .
5.	ladry	ness	. . . .

6. brefy   ly   . . . .
7. fluny   ous   . . . .
8. sepoy   ed   . . . .
9. sacety   able   . . . .
10. nluply   ful   . . . .
11. nofsogry es   . . . .

RULE V—*ie* AND *ei*

Name. . . . . .Date. . . . .

I. On the back of this sheet write the *ei* spelling rule. If you cannot spell a word, write it the best that you can.

II. Some of these words are not spelled right. Write them as they should be.

Wrong   *Right*

1. lenient   . . . .
2. conceive   . . . .
3. leiutenant   . . . .
4. decietful   . . . .
5. reciept   . . . .
6. expedeint   . . . .

Wrong   (In these words *ei* is sounded as ā.)   *Right*

1. vien   . . . .
2. siene   . . . .
3. deign   . . . .

III. These are not real words. Make believe that they are. Some of them are wrong. Spell them as the *ie* rule says they should be spelled.

Wrong   *Right*

1. fier   . . . .
2. ciep   . . . .
3. leciek   . . . .
4. gepreil   . . . .
5. jadeihed . . . .

Wrong   (In these words *ei* is sounded as ā.)   *Right*

1. sieb   . . . .
2. netreive . . . .
3. biwiegat . . . .

RULE VI—SOUND OF *i* SPELLED *y*

Name. . . . . .Date. . . . .

I. Write the *i-y* rule for spelling. If you cannot spell a word, write it the best that you can.

II. All of these words have some sound of *i* at the end. Some of them are not spelled right. Write them as they should be.

Wrong   *Right*

1. compli   . . . .
2. duley   . . . .

3. agencie   . . . .
4. vare   . . . .
5. nameley   . . . .
6. enemy   . . . .
7. miserie   . . . .
8. slippere   . . . .
9. laundre   . . . .
10. grocerey   . . . .

III. These words are not real words.   Make believe that they are.   All of them have some sound of *i* at the end.   Some of them are wrong.   Spell them as they should be spelled.

Wrong	*Right*
1. ghi	. . . .
2. glie	. . . .
3. fse	. . . .
4. nubre	. . . .
5. gopley	. . . .
6. laply	. . . .
7. wiksie	. . . .
8. fepribi	. . . .
9. credagie	. . . .
10. psoboprey	. . . .

BIBLIOGRAPHY

1. ARCHER, C. P. "Saving Time in Spelling Instruction." *Journal of Educational Research*, XX, 122-131. September 1929.
2. ASHBAUGH, ERNEST J. *The Iowa Spelling Scales: Their Derivation, Uses, and Limitations.* Public School Publishing Company, Bloomington, Illinois, 1922.
3. BURNHAM, WILLIAM H. "The Hygiene and Psychology of Spelling." *The Pedagogical Seminary*, XIII, 474-501. December 1906.
4. CARROLL, H. A. *Generalization of Bright and Dull Children.* Contributions to Education, No. 439. Bureau of Publications, Teachers College, Columbia University, New York, 1930.
5. COOK, W. A. "Shall We Teach Spelling by Rule?" *The Journal of Educational Psychology*, III, 316-325. June 1912.
6. GATES, ARTHUR I. AND CHASE, ESTHER H. "Methods and Theories of Learning to Spell Tested by Studies of Deaf Children." *The Journal of Educational Psychology*, XVII, 289-300. May 1926.
7. HORN, ERNEST. *A Basic Writing Vocabulary: 10,000 Words Most Commonly Used in Writing.* College of Education, University of Iowa Monographs in Education. University of Iowa, Iowa City, 1926.
8. HORN, ERNEST. "Principles of Methods in Teaching Spelling as Derived from Scientific Investigation." *The Eighteenth Year Book of the National Society for the Study of Education*, Part II, pp. 52-77. Public School Publishing Company, Bloomington, Illinois, February 1919.
9. HORN, ERNEST AND ASHBAUGH, ERNEST J. "The Necessity of Teaching Derived Forms in Spelling." *The Journal of Educational Psychology*, X, 143-151. March 1919.
10. IRMINA, SISTER M. *et al. An Annotated Bibliography of Studies Relating to Spelling.* The Catholic University of America, Educational Research Bulletins, III, 3-56. January 1928.
11. LESTER, JOHN A. "Delimitation of the Spelling Problem." *The English Journal*, VI, 402-411. June 1917.
12. MENDENHALL, JAMES E. *An Analysis of Spelling Errors: A Study of Factors Associated with Word Difficulty.* Bureau of Publications, Teachers College, Columbia University, New York, 1930.
13. SARTORIUS, INA C. *Generalization in Spelling.* Contributions to Educa-

tion, No. 472. Bureau of Publications, Teachers College, Columbia University, New York, 1931.

14. SUZZALLO, HENRY. *The Teaching of Spelling.* Houghton Mifflin Company, Boston, 1913.

15. THORNDIKE, EDWARD L. "The Effect of Changed Data upon Reasoning." *Journal of Experimental Psychology,* V, 33-38. February 1922.

16. THORNDIKE, EDWARD L. "The Need of Fundamental Analysis of Methods of Teaching." *Elementary School Journal,* XXX, 189-191. November 1929.

17. TIDYMAN, W. F. AND JOHNSON, EDITH. "Value of Grouping Words According to Similar Difficulties in Spelling." *Journal of Educational Research,* X, 297-301. November 1924.

18. TURNER, E. A. "Rules Versus Drill in Teaching Spelling." *The Journal of Educational Psychology,* III, 460-461. October 1912.

19. WAGNER, CHARLES A. *An Experimental Study of Grouping by Similarity as a Factor in the Teaching of Spelling.* Doctor's Dissertation, University of Pennsylvania, Philadelphia, 1912.

20. WATSON, ALICE E. "Experimental Studies in the Psychology and Pedagogy of Spelling." Unpublished Doctor's Dissertation, Teachers College, Columbia University, New York, 1926.

VITA

Luella M. King, the author of this study, was born in Hamilton, Minnesota, in 1887. She received her grade school education in a rural school in that state. In 1907 she was graduated from the Chatfield High School at Chatfield, Minnesota. In 1915 she received the two-year diploma from the Winona State Teachers College in Winona, Minnesota. In 1925 she was given the bachelor of science degree at the University of Minnesota and in 1929 the master of arts degree at Teachers College, Columbia University.

She taught in the rural schools of Minnesota from 1907 to 1913. During 1915–1916 she taught in the elementary division of the training department of Winona State Teachers College. The years, 1916 to 1924, were spent in the high school teacher-training departments of Minnesota. During 1925–1928 she served as rural school supervisor for the state of Montana. For two years, 1929 to 1931, she was supervisor of elementary education at Garden City, Long Island. During the summer of 1930 she worked with the Division of Special Problems in the Bureau of Education at Washington, D. C.